Clinging to Faith

Peter D. Bishop

Clinging to Faith

EPWORTH PRESS

0 7162 0507 6

First published in Britain 1996
by Epworth Press
20 Ivatt Way
Peterborough PE3 7PG

Typeset by Regent Typesetting, London
and printed in Great Britain by
Biddles Ltd, Guildford and King's Lynn

For Mark and Helen
and their families

Contents

Spirituality

Conclusion

Preface

Many people today are only just clinging to faith. In recent years it appears to have become increasingly difficult for people who are in the Christian tradition, but who are also deeply influenced by modern critical scholarship in the arts, humanities and social sciences, to feel at home in the churches. After a brief resurgence of Protestant Liberalism in the 1960s the tide of thinking and teaching in the churches has been flowing in the opposite direction. Conservative evangelicals are more likely to be encountered, or to be influential, than are liberal or radical thinkers. The mainstream churches have continued to decline, and the congregations which grow are those of the Pentecostal or independent house-church type in which scholarship – even biblical scholarship – is eschewed and in which little or no notice is taken of intellectual traditions. What goes on in the churches is less and less likely to engage the minds of people outside or on the fringes of them.

This is happening at a time when educational standards have risen considerably and when, for example, the number of people enjoying university-level education has increased very rapidly. The fact that the education of the clergy and full-time ministers has not only failed to keep pace with this, but in many cases has declined at precisely the time when the laity has become better educated, is one of the curiosities of late twentieth-century Christianity.[1] It may also seem perverse that when university students show an interest in religion (and only a small minority does) it will be the less thoughtful kinds of Christianity with which they associate.

Yet there are still many thoughtful people who wish to explore a religious interpretation of life and to practise in some form a Christian life-style. It is, alas, difficult to find places where that can be done with intellectual integrity. My sympathy with people in that tradition has grown with the years and with experience. After seven years in the Church of South India and a period of pastoral work in British churches, I moved more than twenty years ago to an academic job, teaching and researching in the history of religions in a large and lively Humanities Department of a British polytechnic which became a university. A return to pastoral ministry in a Methodist university church brought into sharper focus the problems inherent in attempting to speak from the texts of what for most is an increasingly obscure biblical tradition to modern, educated, intelligent people. Is it still possible at that level to relate the traditions to a wider intellectual world?

It was in attempting to answer that question for myself that I wrote the reflections that follow, on themes which span a large part of the Christian year. The challenge of attempting to make something relevant out of the texts was a demanding one, and it raises the question of why every chapter save one in this book is concerned in some degree with the exposition of biblical passages. The Bible does not always provide the most suitable starting point for the discussion of a modern issue, and many of the themes dealt with here could very well be treated comprehensively and intelligently on some other basis. Yet the Bible is the set of texts to which Christians are committed. It is inextricably bound up with the life of the church both historically and in the present. Passages from the Bible are read in churches Sunday by Sunday; sermons are expected to be expositions of biblical passages; group Bible study remains a regular activity in churches of all kinds. So whatever the theme being addressed, if it is addressed in the context of a Christian community reference to biblical material is inevitable. The challenge is in discovering whether biblical material can be related to modern intellectual and social contexts in ways that make it meaningful for modern, Western, women and men.The attempt in what follows is to present an understanding of Christian faith as open-minded (one of the chief characteristics of 'liberalism' in the late eighteenth and early nineteenth centuries); politically radical; willing to learn from other faiths; and engaging seriously with texts of Old and New Testaments.

I am indebted to those at Victoria Methodist Church, Bristol, who encouraged this venture, and especially to Sarah Ball, whose help with the manuscript of this book has been considerable and without whose encouragement it would not have appeared in print.

Peter D. Bishop

Approaches

1 Nothing Abides

Nothing distress you,
    nothing afright you,
everything passes,
    God will abide.
Patient endeavour
    accomplishes all things;
who God possesses
    needs nought beside.

'Everything passes, God will abide.' The hymn is by St Teresa of Avila, and it expresses a central religious idea.[1] Everything passes. Try as we might, we cannot cling to the things that attract us: youth, beauty, money, possessions, even relationships. We try to hold on to them; we pretend that they are permanent; but they slip through our grasp and are gone. 'Everything passes; all is denied.' Anyone who knows anything about Eastern religions will detect here more than a hint of Buddhist teaching. At the heart of Buddhism is the acknowledgment that everything is impermanent. We cannot cling to people or possessions, because they and we are changing all the time. And because we cannot hold on, we have to learn to let go.

St Teresa was firmly in the Christian tradition, of course. A Spanish Carmelite nun and mystic in the sixteenth century, her life spanned the momentous years of the Reformation and Catholic Reformation. A contemporary and friend of St John of the Cross, she made a considerable contribution to Christian writing on prayer and spirituality. Teresa seems to have been very aware of her own – and perhaps of everybody else's – mortality. It was in the light of that awareness that her faith was formed and expressed. 'Everything passes, God will abide.'

The Bible has a similar understanding. Psalm 103 expresses a starkly realistic view of mortality:

As for man, his days are like grass;
he flourishes like a flower of the field;
for the wind passes over it, and it is gone,
and its place knows it no more.

One of the great themes of religion – all religion – is how to handle mortality. What are we to make of the great mystery that lies beyond our sight and our understanding? St Teresa's generation had that more visibly before them than we do. Yet for us, too, death, the death of other people, of loved ones, is one of those great crises that sometimes leave us bitter and resentful; but sometimes they wake us up to reality. 'Everything passes, all is denied.' I didn't know the words. I had never heard of St Teresa. But it was the thought she was expressing that formed the basis of my own religious understanding.

I had a brother, who was two years older than I. We were very close to each other. We had had our scraps when we were younger, but we came to admire each other. And surprisingly, I liked him very much. I say surprisingly because he was always so incredibly good at everything. Blond and blue-eyed, he was the original blue-eyed boy. He was good at school work and a good sportsman. Teachers enthused over him, and frequently told me how hard I would have to work if I were to keep up with him. He was hugely popular with other boys. And girls loved him. As a younger teenager – fourteen or so – I watched with amazement and not a little envy the procession of what looked to me like extraordinarily beautiful and incredibly sophisticated girls (they were all of sixteen years old) who came and went, never threw so much as a glance at me, but gazed adoringly at him.

But we became good friends. We were both part of the National Service generation. My later interests in Gandhi, non-violence, and such things were then totally undeveloped, and it did not occur to either of us that we should do other than join up when the time came. We both decided to join the RAF. If

we were to be in the RAF, it seemed to us, then we had better
fly; and if we were going to fly, surely it was better to be a pilot
than to have somebody else do the driving. So in turn we both
volunteered, and were accepted, for pilot training. Colin went
just one year before me, and by the time my turn came he had
left for the United States for further flying training.

I was just eighteen. Looking back from a much greater age,
that now seems so young. It is still something of a shock to look
at first-year undergraduates and to think of what we were
expected to do at the same age. We knew that flying could be
dangerous, and perhaps that was why it was surrounded by a
feeling of glamour. There were stories and jokes and songs that
made light of the danger, and so tried somehow to domesticate
it. Marching back from drill we would sing to the tune of 'John
Brown's Body':

They're trying to find the WAAF who put the parachute in
   its pack,
And he ain't going to fly no more.
Glory, glory, what a hell of a way to die . . .
And he ain't going to fly no more.

At eighteen and a half I became an acting Pilot Officer, with
a blue line around my sleeve so thin I am sure it could not have
been seen from six feet away. But to us, it was really something.
I was told that I was to go overseas, to the then Southern
Rhodesia, for flying training, and that meant that Colin and I
would not meet for several months more, after ten months without seeing each other. I still have a letter that my brother wrote
to me at that time.

I had been looking forward to seeing you again as soon as I
got home, and I have been really missing all the things we
used to do together. I have been getting an idea of what it is
like not to have a brother, for however many friends you
have around, it is not the same thing. But it looks as if our
re-union will have to wait a further five or six months after
all. I can imagine us strolling down towards the park again,

only instead of talking about whether or not we'll go for a training run tonight, it will be talking about the most turns we've ever done in a spin, or the time the engine nearly packed up!

We never had that conversation. A month after writing that letter, and still four months short of his twenty-first birthday, he was killed, his plane spinning in to the ground as it came in to land one morning.

It was the most traumatic event of my life. Looking back on it now, I am amazed that there was so little help or advice for an eighteen-year-old, bereft and with very difficult decisions to make. My emotions were mixed. There was a strange sense of surprise. How could that have happened to him, who always did everything so perfectly? But there, when I was at last able to think about it, was one of the lessons. Talent, skill, ability, do not protect us. Everything passes; all is denied. There was also, of course, an enormous sense of loss. He had said in that letter, 'I have been getting an idea of what it is like, not to have a brother.' No, he hadn't. That's what I had to do.

People react to death in different ways. At some time in our lives we all have to come to the point of letting go – please God, not at eighteen, but we all have to do it sometime. Sometimes it leads to bitterness and resentment. Sometimes such a crisis becomes a vehicle for revelation: an experience, bitter as it is, that wakes us up to realities we had not previously glimpsed. For me on the whole, thank God, it was the second of those responses. If it is not possible to cling, to hold on to, to rely on youth, ability, talent, energy, what is it possible to hold on to? 'Everything passes . . . God will abide.'

It is possible to hold on to some kind of meaning, and purpose, and hope, and love, to those qualities which in their way are lesser but more specific words for 'God'. A central part of the spiritual quest is the search for meaning and purpose in a constantly changing world. Oh, not the quoting of an odd text from here or there, as though that could mean something.

But the constant, often agonizing, search for meaning, for hope, for love, in a universe that so often seems devoid of them all.

That's the spiritual quest. That's what religion is about. And if for you the answers have come easily, well I'm sorry, but I think you have the wrong answers. I doubt whether at eighteen I had even heard the name of St Teresa of Avila, but I vaguely glimpsed what she knew:

> Everything passes, all is denied.
> Everything passes, God will abide.

That was the crisis that started me towards the ministry, and towards what for nearly forty years now has been an almost constant desire to investigate, and probe, and question, not only Christian faith, but the faith enshrined in many of the world's great religions.

St Teresa's hymn includes the words:

> Follow Christ freely,
> His love will light you
>
> Love in due measure;
> . . . run to loves call!

Teresa was in a tradition which claims that spirituality begins and ends with the experience of being loved. Not so much with loving, but with receiving love. Not just in loving God and people, but in letting ourselves be loved by God and people. And that can be much more difficult. The author of the *Cloud of Unknowing* (himself unknown, but a fourteenth century English writer) claims that the spiritual path begins with 'a blind stirring of love', an inner light which guides and directs. It is that love, revealed in Christ, that Teresa saw as the illumination through 'life's dark ways'. 'His love will light you.'

There is illumination, an enlightening, an awakening, in true encounters with God that wakes us up to reality, and sheds light on what is otherwise clouded in darkness. I have referred already to flying, so it may be appropriate to mention one of my favourite stories connected with flight. It's the well-known

story of Jonathan Livingston Seagull.[2] Jonathan was an unusual
bird. The other gulls were preoccupied with the usual round of
time-consuming economic tasks, flying out to find food, eating
the food, and looking for more food. Jonathan was an odd ball.
His interest in the market economy was slight, his concern for
his own practical needs minimal. But he was intrigued by the
question asked by seagull philosophers from time immemorial:
what is it to *be* a seagull? Clearly the answer had something to
do with flight. So Jonathan experimented. He climbed higher
and higher into the sky, and tried to dive steeper and faster than
any other gull. He had a number of painful mishaps, tumbling
in a blur of feathers when he lost control. Until one day a
thought struck him like a bolt of lightning. Draw in your wings
like a falcon! With his wings tucked in he dived faster and
faster, reaching speeds no gull had known before. And then he
dived clean through the breakfast flock as it returned from its
mundane tasks. Summoned before the council, Jonathan
expected to be congratulated on his aeronautical expertise.
Instead, he was declared outcast from the flock for his deviant
behaviour.

But he persisted with his experiments in flying. He looped, he
did slow rolls, he dived, he rode the high winds far inland, until
he found himself transported to a new world, where other gulls
could achieve the most amazing feats of control and technique
in their flying. For Jonathan, there had been an illumination, a
waking up, a flash of insight into who he was and what he was
doing which had taken him into other worlds where other gulls
followed the same quest.

In the final verse of her hymn, Teresa writes:

Though you have nothing,
   God is your treasure:
Who God possesses
   needs naught beside.

The analogy of flying leads to just one more illustration. As
a young man I was much taken with the writing of Antoine de

St Exupery, French writer and pioneer airman. In the 1930s he flew mail planes in South America; during the Second World War he joined the Free French Air Force, flying from North Africa, and disappeared while flying over the Mediterranean one day in 1944. His books included *The Little Prince*, *Flight to Arras* and *The Wisdom of the Sands*. In the last of those books he wrote about life in an austere desert kingdom, where discipline and order and effort were required to survive in a hostile environment. The prince who is the main character in the book finally retired, and in retirement wrote frequently to his friend. A phrase which recurred in those letters was: 'Today, I too have pruned my roses.' No longer was he concerned with great affairs of state; with decisions about whether other men should live or die; with sending armies off to war; with pushing out the boundaries of his kingdom. Those things were all in the past. What do you do when those exciting things are gone?

St Teresa suggested:

Though you have nothing,
  He is your treasure:
Who God possesses
  Needs naught beside.

We can let go, and hold on only to God.

St Exupery's prince wrote to his loyal friend, 'Today, I too have pruned my roses.' I have done that which is closest to hand; in which I can find some meaning; and in doing which I might still wake up to some greater reality; be illumined by a greater truth.

There is a Zen Buddhist saying, 'How wonderful, how marvellous, I chop wood and carry water.' I do what is closest to hand. And in doing that, the marvellous thing is that I might suddenly wake up to reality.

That experience, of revelation, or illumination, sometimes comes to people through the cruel accidents of life. But it can come in easier ways. In the things that lie closest to hand we might find the clues to what we are intended to be; to the love that will light us; to the faith burning brightly; to the God who is our treasure.

2 Wrestling with Contradictions

There are some great stories in the book of Genesis. Andrew Lloyd Webber made a musical hit out of *Joseph and the Amazing Technicolor Dreamcoat*, but Genesis contains many other powerful and entertaining stories which also provide reflections on important religious themes. The series of sagas in Genesis put into compelling stories accounts of how the ancestors of the Jews arrived in Palestine, went into Egypt and returned again to their 'promised land'. In the process they discovered their God and their religion, established their culture, and built their moral code.

There is the story of Abraham, the great figure of faith; of Isaac, and his narrow escape from death as a sacrifice; of Joseph and the strange events that sent him into Egypt and preserved him there. Between the stories of Isaac and Joseph comes Jacob.

Jacob was the crafty younger brother who deceived his father, and by trickery grabbed the inheritance of the elder brother. Esau, who had been so cruelly deceived, threatened to kill his brother. Jacob fled for his life. On his journey he came to a shrine and lay down to sleep, using one of the stones of the shrine for a pillow. His sleep was troubled, as one might have expected. He had behaved abominably to his brother; he believed Esau was planning to kill him; he was alone, possibly pursued, and in real trouble. As he slept he dreamed of a ladder, reaching up to heaven, and of the Lord standing beside him promising to protect him. When he woke, he said, 'Truly the Lord is in this place, and I did not know it.' He was awestruck, and said, 'How awesome is this place! This is none other than the house of God . . .' (Gen. 28.16, 17). There was Jacob the deceiver, having a genuine religious experience, struck by awe and wonder in that lonely spot. His immediate response included a kind of religious ritual, as he set up a pillar with the stones, poured oil over it, and made his vow to God.

The story continues with Jacob finding his wife Rachel in the land of the eastern tribes, so that he would not marry a Canaanite woman but find a wife connected with his own family. You know the story. Jacob worked seven years for Rachel and they seemed like a few days, because he loved her. But the trickster was tricked. Laban, his prospective father-in-law had an older, if less beautiful, daughter who also needed a husband, and so he duped Jacob into marrying the wrong girl. He found that by some dreadful mischance he had married Leah, the sister who was 'dull-eyed', instead of Rachel, 'who was beautiful in both face and figure'. So beautiful was she that the next seven years flew by as he lived with Leah and thought of the alluring Rachel (Gen. 29.20, 17).

Finally there comes the third great Jacob story, of his return to his own country. The night before he was due to meet his brother Esau again after so many years, he had another great religious experience, this time depicted in terms of wrestling with a stranger. 'Jacob was left alone, and a man wrestled with him there till daybreak'. Wrestling, no doubt, with his own conscience, and attempting to resolve the fears and conflicts awoken by the prospect of a meeting with his brother.

Throughout the story, Jacob is portrayed as a very realistic person. Abraham sounds more like a kind of idealized ancestor, a type of the tribes and people who came to be Israel. But with Jacob the story is much more realistic. Jacob is crafty, fearful, faint, but also determined and courageous. He is good and he is bad. He is loyal, and he is deceitful. In other words, he is remarkably like most of us. And in that sense he is also a realistic embodiment of the actual Israel. The Israel of history and of the prophets, and the Israel of today. He is not a remote, ideal figure, a plaster saint. He is real life.

Possibly Canaanite in origin, Jacob represents the spirit of a people; and after his great experience by the ford of Jabbok he became not Jacob, but Israel. Unlike Abraham, Jacob is not the ideal righteous man. But as a kind of romantic hero, with many contradictions, he is a very powerful religious figure.

Forget about the Old Testament for a moment, and think about some other great religious figures. Let me introduce you to Siva, sometimes known as Natarajan, 'the Lord of the dance'. Siva is a great representation of God among Hindus. And he is a paradoxical figure. He is both creator and destroyer, because creation and destruction are two parts of the same process. He is good and bad, and both are contained within our own experience and our own personalities. Siva is the great ascetic, and a common portrayal is of him seated in yogic fashion in the Himalayas, naked, with matted hair, absorbed in meditation. He represents self-denial of an extreme form. But he is also a very erotic figure, represented in thousands of shrines around India by the lingam, the slender pillar in the shape of the erect penis, for one of the characteristics of Siva is that he remains at the same time permanently erect and permanently chaste. Is this simply bizarre? I think not. An American scholar of Indian religions, Wendy Doniger O'Flaherty, points out that Siva becomes a mediating principle, helping to resolve conflicts which are in us all but which many forms of religion simply try to repress.

> Among ascetics he is a libertine, and among libertines an ascetic; conflicts which they cannot resolve he simply absorbs into himself, and expresses in terms of other conflicts . . . Mediating characters of this type are essential to all mythologies which deal in contradictions.[1]

The role of great figures in many ancient religious stories is to reconcile opposites. So much of our own lives is deeply coloured by opposites: drought and flood, laughter and tears, joy and sadness, life and death. And in the stories of the great figures of many religions there is that same sense of paradox, although the paradox is in the end resolved. The stories suggest that the great paradoxes of our lives can in the end be incorporated into some meaningful system.

And so the story of Jacob tells of his return to his homeland to face his brother Esau and to resolve the contradictions of his deception, his flight and his prospering in the lands of the east. He sent his wives, his slave-girls, his sons, and everything he had across the river before him, and then he had a strange experience. Genesis tells how: 'After he had sent them across the wadi with all that he had, Jacob was left alone, and a man wrestled with him there till daybreak' (Gen. 32.23, 24). Charles Wesley turned the text into poetry in a hymn:

> Come, O thou traveller unknown,
>   Whom still I hold, but cannot see!
> My company before is gone,
>   And I am left alone with thee;
> With thee all night I mean to stay,
>   And wrestle till the break of day.
>
> I need not tell thee who I am,
>   My misery and sin declare;
> . . . But who I ask thee, who art thou?
> Tell me thy name, and tell me now.

What was Jacob wrestling with? The contradictions of his own character, perhaps. The struggle of good and evil that went on inside him. In the end he clung to the good side of his nature. The man said. 'Let me go, for day is breaking', but Jacob replied, 'I will not let you go unless you bless me' (Gen. 32.26). And so it was. Jacob was changed by that encounter. In the saga the transformation is marked by the change of name, from Jacob to Israel, a name that means 'God strove'. And so the eponymous hero of the story characterizes Israel itself. Israel, which is by no means perfect, its people struggling, disobeying, finding their true self again, and being redeemed.

A similar idea is found in the New Testament, in Mark 14.26–31. The Passover meal is over, and Jesus and his disciples go to the Mount of Olives. Jesus says to the disciples, 'You will all lose faith; for it is written, "I will strike the shepherd and the sheep will be scattered." ' And that provoked

Peter's famous response: 'Everyone else may lose faith, but I will not . . . Even if I have to die with you, I will never disown you.'

It was a critical moment. In her commentary on Mark, Morna Hooker suggests:

> Throughout Mark has stressed the failure of the disciples to comprehend, but they have at least followed him. Now they will fail to do even that.[2]

Yet in advance of Peter's running away, there was his strong denial. 'I will never disown you.' Was he foolish to say that? Like Jacob, was he not also a real human character? And more than that, was he not a man in need of God's grace and support? Simone Weil made a perceptive comment on this when she wrote:

> To say to Christ: 'I will never deny Thee' was to deny him already, for it was supposing the source of faithfulness to be in himself and not in grace.[3]

We are all mixed, ambivalent characters, and all in need of the grace of God. Jacob was a real-life paradox, a mixture of good and bad; so were the disciples; and so are we. The stories of Jesus and his disciples point again to the paradoxes, as does the story of Jacob. We may have the best of intentions; but we cannot always fulfil them.

The story of Jacob who became Israel is the story of the Jewish people, for it contains many paradoxes, some of them of enormous proportions. Jews would say, I think, that they remain faithful to their calling and to the covenant not in order to gain rewards in heaven, nor to avoid difficulties (indeed, the Jewish vocation has often invited difficulties), but simply because God *is*. Such a belief is not always easy to hold on to. We know only too well of the horrors suffered by millions of Jews during the Nazi period. After the war, scratched on the wall of a cellar in Cologne where Jews had hidden from the Nazis were the words:

I believe in the sun, even when it is not shining;
I believe in love, even when feeling it not;
I believe in God, even when He is silent.

Does that not express the gigantic paradox of religious hope?
  In his hymn about wrestling Jacob, Charles Wesley moves on
to picture Jacob crying out to his assailant:

Speak, or thou never hence shalt move,
   And tell me if thy name is Love.

'Tis Love! 'Tis Love! Thou diedst for me!
   I hear thy whisper in my heart;
The morning breaks, the shadows flee,
   Pure, universal love thou art;
To me, to all, thy mercies move;
   Thy nature and thy name is Love.

So may it be for us.

3 Christian Existentialism

Journeys play a large part in religion, and in the lives of many of us today. They may not be the most fascinating subject for conversation, but they are surely one of the most common. Bend your ear to the conversation of groups of people at a social gathering, or a wedding or funeral, and whatever the occasion that has brought people together, you can be sure that journeys will be in people's minds. 'Did you come down the M5 then?' 'No, we decided to use the A38 instead.' 'Oh, so you came via Stroud? Wasn't that slower?'

And so it can go on, and on. Such conversation might simply represent the banality of our lives, or perhaps it is just an attempt to express our own individuality. In a time of increasingly centralized political power, achieved through the neutering of those traditional balances to our democratic system, the local authorities and the unions; and in a time of increasingly remote economic power, when multi-national companies determine national economic programmes, it may be that control of our own individual vehicles has become an important symbol of our independence.

Which thoughts occurred to me when once again I dipped briefly into Jean Paul Sartre. Sartre, the great French existentialist philosopher. Sartre, scourge of establishments, of those who wield power for their own benefit. Sartre, the author of the occasional *bon mot* which lives in the memory: *L'enfer, c'est les autres* [hell is other people] – was he right about that?

Sartre's philosophy was in part a protest against powerful ideologies. In the 1930s and 1940s he was an implacable opponent of fascism, expressed by the Nazis in Germany and in Franco's Spain, where the all-powerful state would brook no opposition. He saw the oppressive power of the state expressed also in the armed services, recruiting more and more people into a world in which personal autonomy disappeared altogether. Against that background Sartre emphasized personal freedom and choice, repudiating the tyrannies of states, and economic powers, and of all those who squeeze individual freedom out of life, alienating the people from the world in which they have to live. It was in that context that he concentrated on what it is to be a person, an individual, rejecting the great overriding ideologies and belief systems, and concentrating instead on the individual's own experience.

Which brings us back to journeys, and the attempt to assert our own individuality through them. Journeys, of various kinds, have long had great religious significance. Chaucer's *Canterbury Tales* remind us of the liveliness and turbulence of pilgrim journeys in late mediaeval England, with his stories of the thirty-one pilgrims who set off from the Tabard Inn, at Southwark, to visit the shrine of Thomas à Becket at Canterbury. Pilgrimage remains popular. More than five million people flock to Lourdes every year, and other pilgrim centres attract large numbers of people who presumably expect their journeys to lead them to greater faith.

In the Bible, journeys are often related to faith.

Abraham set out on his journey from the ancient land of Babylon (modern Iraq) and came to be regarded as the father-figure of faith for all the three great religions which began in the Middle East – Judaism, Christianity, and Islam. The writer of the Letter to the Hebrews says of Abraham: 'By faith Abraham obeyed the call to leave his home for a land which he was to receive as a possession; he went away without knowing where he was to go' (Heb. 11.8).

Abraham was a hero of faith because he did not know where he was going! He had to live without some great overarching plan, and take one day at a time as he pursued his journey into the unknown.

There were occasions when the prophets of Israel spoke about journeys. Some well-known words of Jeremiah were addressed to people who were about to embark upon a journey (Jer. 31.31–34). It was a journey into exile. He was speaking to people who had to leave their homeland in the sixth century BC and go to that same part of the world from which Abraham had come, to Babylon. There, by the waters of Babylon, they sat down and wept when they remembered Zion, their homeland. Jeremiah had reminded them that in the contemporary experience of everyday God would be with them, no longer as the God whose law was evident in life all around them, but as the God who spoke in their hearts, and so could still be known in their living experience. The journey into exile was also a journey of faith.

Journeys also feature on the New Testament, and not only in stories of Paul's travels around the Mediterranean world. Consider Mark's dramatic introduction to the ministry of Jesus in the first chapter of his Gospel. According to the text: 'Jesus was walking by the sea of Galilee when he saw Simon and his brother Andrew at work with casting-nets in the lake; for they were fishermen. Jesus said to them, "Come, follow me, and I will make you fishers of men"' (Mark 1.16f.).

Then he came upon James and John. 'At once he called them; and they left their father Zebedee in the boat with the hired men and followed him.' Look again at those two verses. Is there something curious about them? Would people see a virtual stranger passing by, hear him say those words, and immediately leave everything to follow him? Or is the text a dramatic heightening of the incident, so as to emphasize something important about becoming a follower of Jesus?

Journeys of faith do not always require movement over great distances. The beginnings of Mark's Gospel suggest that Christian faith itself involves a journey. It is a matter of following Christ much more than simply following a code or believing a creed. It seems to suggest that Christian faith is existential. It is marked by the unpredictable, by the need for a person to respond to unique events as they happen, and to take responsibility for his or her own life.[1] It also implies that Christian faith can only be fully understood as it is lived.

Regarded as a collection of doctrines or as an ideology, it inevitably remains both peculiar and dead.

The disciples' calling began with an invitation to make a decision: the decision to leave their no doubt comfortable and happy lives and to set out on a hazardous journey in following Jesus. For those disciples their decision did involve a number of journeys around Galilee and to Jerusalem. But chiefly it led to a journey of faith. They engaged in some travelling around Palestine. There was some physical movement, although in that sense it was not an epic journey. But their movement, their journey, in terms of who they were and how they saw their lives in relation to the systems and people around them, that was great.

Notice that in the brief but compelling passage from Mark the introduction to Jesus was made not in terms of learn, think about, repeat after me, but in the abrupt words 'follow me'. The invitation was to begin a journey in which they would work out what it meant to have Christian faith. It did not begin for those disciples with absolute certainties on which they could bank. It began with a risk, with 'freedom to choose and to act in unique and unpredictable ways . . . accompanied by a sense of urgency and anxiety'.[2] The present moment, and the decisions required by it, was what mattered.

They followed Jesus all the way to Gethsemane and Calvary. No doubt they noticed, in those two most desolate spots, that even for Jesus there were no certainties. Jesus, too, had his doubts which surfaced in the most troubled waters at the end of his ministry.

In Gethsemane, he pleaded: 'Father, let this cup [this suffering] pass me by; nevertheless, not my will, but yours be done.' And on the cross he asked, 'My God, my God, why have you forsaken me?' Jesus had to dispense with absolute certainties and accept risks in order to live by faith. And so do we.

In chapter six of John's Gospel there is the story of the feeding of the five thousand, which is followed by a fascinating series of exchanges. Jesus refused to pander to the demands of the crowd for more miracles and marvels. That, of course, is what the religious crowds really love, and what religious crowds still want today. But instead of satisfying their demands, Jesus began to speak about the loaves as though they were something symbolic, standing for the 'bread of life', the life of risk and adventure and faith and commitment to which he called people. Even his disciples were put out by that: ' . . . on hearing, many of his disciples exclaimed, "This is more than anyone can stand" . . . From that moment, many of his disciples drew back and no longer went about with him' (John 6.60, 66).

Jesus turned to the inner group, the remaining twelve, and asked them wistfully: 'Do you also want to leave?' Peter replied: 'Lord, to whom shall we go? Your words are the words of eternal life' (John 6.67f.).

They were probably not too sure about it. But they recognized that following Jesus involved a deliberate letting go of what for most people passes as security, including even religious security. So it does for all of us who would attempt to follow Jesus. The German theologian Jürgen Moltmann once said that Christian tradition 'is not to be understood as a handing on of something that has to be preserved, but as an event which summons the dead and the godless to life'.[3]

Do you see the threads that connect it all? There is a proper Christian existentialism, traced back to the Danish philosopher Kierkegaard, who remarked that when he spoke about doctrine everybody commended him, but that when he applied Christian faith to everyday life 'it is just as though I had exploded existence – the *scandal* is there at once'.[4] Following Jesus can require us to stand against the over-arching systems of domination and control, the systems and ideologies – even religious ideologies – which depersonalize individuals and societies. Following Jesus demands that we take our own decisions, with freedom to choose in an unpredictable world. We then accept Christian faith, not as an object to be admired, but as a reality to be discovered as we risk answering the call to 'Follow me'.

4 On Being an Intelligent Christian

It is always a delight to be with students, to share their enthusiasms and enjoy their laughter. And part of the privilege of having been a university chaplain was the opportunity of encouraging students to think about as well as to practise a faith. One regrettable feature of the student scene in the 1990s, however, is that many students who hold to some kind of Christian faith appear to do so in order to avoid thinking. It is a paradox. At the time when people are regularly attending lectures and seminars, being invited to consider new ideas and handle new concepts, one might expect that they would also welcome the challenge of re-thinking religious ideas, of looking critically at received texts, of thinking as hard about their faith as they do about their area of study. Alas, it is rarely so. The idea that it is possible to be an intelligent person and a Christian seems to be rejected as firmly by those with a religious faith as it is by those without one.

Years ago, long before most students of today's generation were born, there was a fierce and public theological debate, carried on not only in books and libraries but also in the popular press, and on television and radio. A popular debate, not on law and order, or taxation, or education, but on theology. Imagine that!

It was during the 1960s. John Robinson, a New Testament scholar who was also at the time Bishop of Woolwich, strayed from his own discipline into the more abstract areas of theology, and wrote a book called *Honest to God*.[1] By putting into a popular form the ideas of such people as Rudolph Bultmann, Paul Tillich, and Dietrich Bonhoeffer, Robinson created a great fuss. Clearly, people were surprised to learn what it is that is said by academic theologians, and became greatly excited, whether they were for or against, when they were told. Some suggested that John Robinson should be dismissed from the office of bishop for daring to air thoughts that apparently should only be thought in the academy. I recall a distinguished church historian saying in private conversation that if Robinson were dismissed 'all it would prove is that you cannot at the same time be an intelligent person and a bishop in the Church of England'.

Never mind about the bishops. They must look after themselves. Can *we* be intelligent people and Christians? Many would assume not. Yet for university students, of all people, it is a proper question to ask.

In the Book of Proverbs, wisdom is commended as a gift of God. Proverbs asks:

> How long will you simple fools be content with your
>   simplicity?
> If only you would respond to my reproof, I would fill you
>   with my spirit . . . (Prov. 1.22f.)

In Wisdom literature God's gifts and thoughtful understanding go together. The opposite there of 'wise' is not 'ignorant' but 'empty', 'thick-headed' or even 'evil'. An important distinction is drawn between the accumulation of facts and the gaining of understanding. The fool may know a great many facts, but he has not thought hard enough about how they relate and what they mean to have found the key to life's meaning. There is no commendation there of a religion that is simply empty-headed. The New Testament takes a similar view.

Think if you will of the first chapter of John's Gospel. It is a passage most often read around Christmas time, but it is not a reading that can only be read to an accompaniment of candles, and carols, and turkey. Perhaps we associate some readings too closely with particular seasons. There is a more universal application of the words John wrote there about the divine 'word': 'So the Word became flesh ; he made his home among us, and we saw his glory, such glory as befits the Father's only Son, full of grace and truth' (John 1.14).

The Greek word *logos* is used here for what has existed from the beginning of time. In almost all English translations it is rendered 'word', although that is not its literal meaning. There is a perfectly good, but different, way of translating 'word' into Greek. What *logos* means is more an intelligible self-disclosure that can be understood and appropriated by people. And the use of *logos* for the self-disclosure of the otherwise unknowable God reflects much wider cultural, philosophical, and theological contexts than those of first-century Judaism and Christianity alone. John is suggesting, by the use of that word, that the disclosure which occurs in Jesus is linked with what is known to Greek philosophers and in Hebrew wisdom literature. That knowledge of God through Jesus Christ is all of a piece with true wisdom in other times and places, and part of the wisdom which undergirds all profound human thought.

In one of his hymns, Charles Wesley celebrated wisdom in the words:

Wisdom divine, who tells the price
    Of wisdom's costly merchandise?
. . . Happy the man who wisdom gains,
    Thrice happy who his guest retains:
He owns, and shall for ever own,
    Wisdom, and Christ, and heaven are one.

According to Proverbs, wisdom cries aloud in the open air; but simple fools do not hear, and are content with their simplicity.

University life should be a great experience, of friendships, and parties, and fun, but also an experience of encountering new worlds of knowledge and the sheer excitement of new ideas, the challenge of intellectual pursuits. And that ought to connect with *logos*, with Christian faith and understanding and practice. It is possible to be intelligent people and to be Christians; for the intellect and faith to inform each other. To do that might be one aim of student life, as well as a constant aim of church life. When I was a chaplain I used to ensure that displayed outside my church were deliberately provocative posters, intended to make people think, and to provide a contrast with the biblical texts which sometimes adorn church notice boards. One presented to the passer-by some words of Raimundo Panikkar: 'Only on the journey is God to be found'.[2] More provocatively, another displayed words of an early Christian writer and thinker, known as Dionysius: 'If someone, seeing God, knew what he saw, he did not see God'.[3]

That's worth reflecting upon at any time. Certainly people going by on the bus or sitting in their cars in a traffic jam did notice the unusual messages we presented to the world. Many people, when told what it was I represented in Bristol, responded by saying: 'Oh, is that the church that has the interesting posters outside?' As a university church it seemed to me we should try to help people think.

But there are obstacles in the way. Some Christians try very hard to keep knowledge and faith apart. Many like to hide from intellectual challenges to their faith. If you mix with a variety of Christian students, you might notice that ostriches are very fashionable. Indeed, you will hardly be able to walk down some roads without tripping over the elevated rump of a Christian ostrich, head buried securely in the ground.

It can be attractive to pretend that serious intellectual questions do not arise when dealing with matters of faith, and it can be the easier option. Feed the emotions; be nice to people; and don't raise difficult questions. Wouldn't that do very nicely? It's a perilous trap, and many people fall into it. But let us not forget that great numbers of people have fled the churches, and will continue to flee, simply because they find what goes on to be mentally, intellectually, unsatisfying. We desperately need an intelligent application of Christian faith. It is true that churches sometimes fail to attract people because they are dull, or unwelcoming, or drab. In spite of that, there can be little doubt that the massive loss of people from the churches in the last thirty or forty years has to do chiefly with belief; people do not find credible what they think it is that Christians believe.

In a university context, thinking about faith, reading texts critically, looking sceptically at religious institutions, should be perfectly normal and acceptable things to do. But turn the phrase 'intelligent person' into 'intellectual' and the problem is immediately apparent. In English life the word intellectual is suspect. Accuse a politician of being an intellectual, and people are much less likely to say, 'oh good, he's bright enough to understand the problems he claims to be dealing with', than they are to regard him – or her – with deep suspicion. Partly that may be, as Raymond Williams suggests, that in Britain there has been a tendency to oppose 'social or political arguments based on theory or on rational principle'.[4] Yet what students and staff do in universities is to apply rational principles to whatever subject they study, and certainly they have to be acquainted with the major theories in their field. Why not dare to do the same with religious practice and belief?

Part of the resistance to doing that, I guess, is really a lack of confidence in the way our beliefs and practices have been formulated. We are wary of getting into arguments we think we shall not win. Rather than set out an intelligent basis for our faith, we prefer to rely on experience: 'I know what I feel, and so I am sure of my faith.' That is now an immensely popular view among Christians. It has its appeal. For those of the traditional student age-groups it fits with other parts of life outside lecture halls and seminar rooms. Falling in and out of love; discovering new relationships; loosening old ties and creating new ones; responding strongly to music and poetry; all are full of powerful emotional currents. Religion also needs emotion: something of the feel of vibrant or beautiful music; poetic insights that are not simply rational; and at least a little of the breathtaking feeling of falling in love. But if it is to be more than a youthful fling, it requires something else. It needs to be related to traditions of thought, and to be put into an intellectual framework.

That takes us back to the important New Testament concept

of the *logos*, the self-disclosure of God in a rational and ordered world. The *logos*, the Word which has existed from the beginning of time, and which has made God known. That divine self-disclosure of the otherwise unknowable God reflects wide cultural, philosophical and religious backgrounds. And it has to do with action as well as with abstract thought.

Christian belief asserts that God revealed himself supremely in Jesus Christ. But it does not deny that God might also have revealed himself elsewhere. Indeed, the association of Jesus of Nazareth with the divine *logos* is itself a claim that what Christians know of God is consistent with what has been known in previous times and in other places. Setting our religious faith in an intellectual context will enable us to relate it to much wider cultural and intellectual traditions than those of conventionally Christian Europe. The Word that became flesh in Jesus might speak to us also through the writings of the great religious thinkers of India, the Chinese classics, and the austere words spoken through Muhammad, as it will inevitably connect with what has been uttered in the life of Judaism. There is a beautiful prayer in an Indian scripture which has been adapted into our own baptism service, via the Church of South India. The prayer asks:

> From the unreal lead me to the real;
> from darkness lead me to light;
> from death lead me to immortality.[5]

That is a prayer of people of all faiths.

When we read the New Testament, however, we are likely to be struck by something more than that deep religious sense. We shall also notice how strong is the sense of community and how insistent the call to social action. In connection with that, we might notice that the British suspicion of intellectuals is partly rooted in a fear that such people wish to question comfortable traditions which preserve the privileges of a small minority. Raymond Williams, writing about negative attitudes to intellectuals, commented on the development of opposition to groups engaged in intellectual work because they 'had acquired some independence from established institutions, in the church and in politics, and . . . were certainly seeking and asserting such independence through the 18th, 19th and 20th centuries'.[6]

To marry intellectual traditions to Christian faith is to bring together the best of both, and to relate them to authentic New Testament teaching. The eternal Word revealed in Jesus is concerned very much with justice and righteousness, with the poor and disadvantaged of society, with peace and community. It is also critical of received traditions, enquiring in matters of religious belief and practice, and open to new ideas. Christian faith must engage with the intellectual life of the nation if Christianity is not to degenerate into a series of sectarian and largely irrelevant emotional stimuli. It also has to engage with wider intellectual concerns if it is to proclaim a message of social concern.

That has to relate to what the Bible calls wisdom: the divine *logos*, the self-disclosure of God in a world in which people do indeed think, and enquire, and agonize over what it is to believe.

> . . . give your attention to wisdom,
> and your mind to understanding;
> cry out for discernment and invoke understanding;
>   seek for her as silver and dig for her as buried treasure;
> then you will understand the fear of the Lord and attain to
>   the knowledge of God (Prov. 2.2–6).

> . . . the Word became flesh; he made his home among us, and we saw his glory, such glory as befits the Father's only Son, full of grace and truth (John 1.14).

Beliefs

5 Believing in God

Apparently, a large number of people, even in our modern secular society, believe in God. In a census of religious belief and practice carried out in 1990, only 27% declared themselves to be atheists or agnostics. Those saying they were Christians comprised 65% of the population, although regular church-goers amounted to only 10%.[1] So do all of the 65%, plus many of the 8% belonging to 'non-trinitarian or non-Christian religions', believe in God? They would probably say so, in response to such a simple question. But is the question, 'do you believe in God?' a useful one to ask? It is a question we might not think of asking in a church, on the assumption that only people who believe in God go to church. But even if everyone in a congregation were to answer 'yes' to the question, the replies would tell us very little. It would be much more interesting, and the answers much more revealing, if we were to ask instead, 'what do you mean when you say that you believe in God?' 'What kind of God do you believe in?' Believers can mean quite different things from one another when they say 'I believe in God'. And within many congregations there would be people who would want to hedge their bets and preface any answer by saying, 'it depends what you mean by God.' Of course it does.

What is it to believe in God? We could begin a search for an answer by looking at Psalm 139, which is thoughtful, reflective, and surprisingly mystical for a Psalm. The writer says of God:

> O Lord, you have searched me out, and known me:
>   you know when I sit or when I stand
>   you comprehend my thoughts long before.[2]

At the beginning of this psalm there is a strong emphasis on
the inescapable nature of God. Whatever we do, wherever we
go, we cannot escape from whatever it is that the word 'God'
means. Notice a few more lines from the same psalm:

Where shall I go from your spirit:
  or where shall I flee from your presence?
If I ascend into heaven you are there:
  if I make my bed in the grave you are there also.
If I spread out my wings towards the morning:
  or dwell in the uttermost parts of the sea,
Even there your hand shall lead me:
  and your right shall hold me.

God is inescapable because he is everywhere. He is not an
object among other objects in the world who could be hidden,
or could hide, somewhere. God is what is encountered in the
depths of our own experiences: encountered perhaps in illness,
if it is the kind of illness that makes us think about our own
future; encountered in bereavement, when we are brought up
against the temporary and changing nature of life, and have to
ask whether in that experience there is any meaning or purpose.
God is inescapable, because God is the meaning and purpose of
the universe itself.

Does that seem to be a strange way of thinking about God?
If it does, then we need to remind ourselves that it has a long
Christian history, going right back to the early church fathers
in the first few centuries of Christian faith. Many of those early
Christian thinkers agreed that what we mean by 'God' cannot
simply be *a* person among other persons; *a* being among other
beings, only a little more powerful than the rest.

Thomas Aquinas, one of the greatest thinkers of the
mediaeval church, once wrote that 'God is in the world as the
soul is in the body.' That might be a helpful analogy. What do
we mean when we speak about the soul? Presumably we don't
mean something that could be stumbled upon in the middle of
a dissection – 'oh look, here's the soul!' I take it that what we

mean when we speak about the soul is much more like that part of a human personality which gives meaning, direction and purpose to life. That intangible something which adds to the composition of flesh and bones and blood and mind, and provides it with a sense both of wholeness and of meaning. Think of a person learning music. There is at first all that effort to learn notation, and so to be able to understand all the funny dots and marks on paper (and the dots and marks are not themselves music, are they?) Then the effort to relate those to, say, a piano keyboard, or to the bowing and fingering of a violin. Then follows all the effort required to be able to make the right connections, to read the writing off the page and produce it as sounds from the instrument, thinking all the time of what you are doing. But if your skills develop, there will come a moment when that part of the process will be almost automatic. It will be second nature to read the notation and reproduce what it signifies on the instrument. At that point the accomplished performer can begin to concentrate not on the mechanics but on the meaning of the music, and if really talented perhaps to become the means of communicating the meaning and intention of what was in the composer's mind to the audience.

That is one way of thinking about the soul, as what it is that gives meaning and purpose to what is otherwise mechanical and predictable. Think about that for a moment in relation to God. 'God is in the world as the soul is in the body.' God is not a separate object, like a soul that could be discovered in an anatomy class. God is not a separate object, like notes on the paper, or keys on the keyboard, by themselves lifeless and unmoving. God is what it is that gives meaning and purpose and direction to the whole. And that is something which Christian theologians – some of them, at least – have always said about God. It is the way some of the early church fathers spoke about God. It is the way the sixth-century writer who used the name Dionysius spoke about God. It is the way Paul Tillich in the twentieth century has spoken about God.

A contemporary Christian philosopher, D. Z. Phillips, complains that many critics of Christianity today assume that thinking of God as though he were simply another person is the normal Christian belief, and so they enjoy knocking down something that cannot be defended. He asks:

> Should a believer be expected to produce his God? The philosophers' demand is ironic, because anything that could be produced would not be God. God is not a being among beings; not an additional fact to those facts already known. God is not hidden, in this sense, and therefore could not be produced, like a rabbit out of a hat.[3]

God is the meaning, the soul, the existence of the world. So, where shall I go from your spirit: or where shall I flee from your presence?

How is that reflected in the New Testament? The first chapter of John's Gospel claims that, 'No one has ever seen God . . .' God is mysterious, or in theological language, he is transcendent. But John added: 'God's only Son, he who is nearest to the Father's heart, he has made him known' (John 1.18). It is because of that belief that the Gospel claims its title of 'the good news'. The Gospels convey the good news that the mysterious, transcendent God has made himself known in the person of Jesus Christ. But notice what John says and does not say: No one has ever seen God. God's only Son, he has made him known. That is the orthodox Christian position. Informed Christians do not claim that God and Jesus or Christ are interchangeable terms, with precisely the same meaning. The orthodox Christian position is expressed clearly by Paul: 'God was in Christ, reconciling the world to himself' (II Cor. 5.9). Notice that he says 'God was in Christ', not 'God was (or is) Christ', but 'God was in Christ'. The New Testament writers distinguish between the mysterious, transcendent God on the one hand and Christ on the other; between God and Jesus of Nazareth.

Popular Christianity does not always do that. Hymns conspicuously fail to do so. The words 'Jesus' and 'God' come to be used interchangeably, as though they mean the same thing. Orthodox Christians believe that God is revealed in Jesus; but that is not the same thing as believing that God is Jesus. Christians are as convinced as Jews and Muslims that there is only one God. William Temple, an impeccably orthodox Anglican archbishop, wrote of John 1.18:

> He (Jesus) does not reveal all that is meant by the word God. There ever remains the unsearchable abyss of Deity. But he reveals what it vitally concerns us to know; he reveals God as Father.[4]

It is in Jesus that God may be glimpsed. But Christians should not make the mistake of believing that 'Jesus' and 'God' are interchangeable terms. Jesus did not claim to be God: indeed, the New Testament texts show him being very careful not to do so.[5] And the too easy identification of Jesus and God encourages the unhelpful view that God is a kind of superman, an individual like us only more powerful, who will fulfil our desires, do what we ask, and allow himself to be manipulated by our prayers. It is not so. God, the meaning and the purpose of our lives and the life of our world, speaks through Jesus. But not everything about God can be expressed by that word.

Yet William Temple was right in saying that 'Jesus reveals what it vitally concerns us to know; he reveals God as Father'. The picture of God which is shown to us in the life and teaching of Jesus is one which is dominated by love. A classic statement about God occurs in the First Letter of John, where it says that:

> Everyone who loves is a child of God and knows God, but the unloving know nothing of God, for God is love . . .
> God has never been seen by anyone, but if we love one another, he himself dwells in us.
> God is love; he who dwells in love is dwelling in God, and God in him (I John 4.7, 8; 12, 16).

God is discovered in loving relationships. Our awareness of God develops and grows as we participate in the divine love through our own expressions of love to those around us. God is not a superperson who exists in order to respond to our manipulation of him, but a process of love in which we may participate and in which we find the meaning and purpose of our lives. The power of God is not the power of a magician, but the power of suffering love. That is why the particular revelation of God cherished and passed on in the Christian tradition is one that focusses on the Jesus who lives for others, loves without limit, and in consequence is willing to accept in himself the suffering that unguarded love can so easily bring. The picture of God which we find in the New Testament centres upon Jesus demonstrating his care for the ill and the injured and the despised; upon Jesus in his terror and his faithfulness in the garden of Gethsemene; upon Jesus in his agony on the cross. The God who is revealed in Jesus is a God of love. We may think of God sharing with us in our sufferings and grieving with us in our sorrows, but also providing the creativity of love as an ocean in which we may play and upon which we make our journeys. We believe in God, whose love is our resource, our support, and our joy.

6 Creative Spirit

How do you describe what you cannot see? We don't have to do it very often, and in any case we might think it is best left to poets. Could we describe our feelings, so that someone else would really know what they mean to us? Even when we are upset, or lonely, or isolated? And could we describe it if something entirely new happened to us, something we had never experienced before?

That was said to be the situation of a group of people described in the New Testament. The disciples had been through a series of shocks and a number of new experiences. The previous great festival in Jerusalem – the Passover – had began in hope. But just as the festival was coming to its climax, things went badly wrong. Jesus was arrested, and his followers all forsook him and fled. It must have seemed to them that their hopes were at an end.

Then came the extraordinary experiences we know as the resurrection. In the words of the Gospels, the followers of Jesus 'trembled with amazement', 'were afraid', and were 'filled with awe and great joy'. All those things happened while they were in Jerusalem for the Passover festival. Seven weeks later, to people whose lives were measured out in festivals, came Pentecost. In modern Judaism Pentecost – now known as Shavu'ot – comes fifty days after the beginning of Passover, and commemorates the revelation of God at Sinai, and also therefore the giving of the Torah, or 'law'.

In Jewish terms, Passover was and is the great festival of freedom, of deliverance, of salvation, recalling how the Hebrews in Egypt were led out of captivity. Shavu'ot is the festival of God's revelation of himself, in the fire and smoke of Sinai and in the giving of the law. The festivals of Passover and Pentecost serve in part to put into dramatized form the mysterious acts by which God communicated something of himself to his people.

But how do you describe something entirely new, for which there are no conventional terms? Sometimes you have to go back to the traditions, and use the words and symbols that everybody knows. The story of the deliverance from Egypt which informs the Passover celebration includes mention of a strong east wind that drove back the waters, and allowed the slaves to escape. The Pentecost celebration of the giving of the law included the accounts of Moses going up the mountain to meet the God who was not seen, but whose presence was indicated by peals of thunder and flashes of lightning.

How do you describe what you do not see? You use those great symbols of the power and the presence of God, wind and fire. In the biblical narrative wind is regarded as something mysterious, and so in that respect is a fitting symbol of the unseen God. In the days before weather forecasts people didn't know where the wind came from or where it was going, but they felt its power.[1] Fire was an even more potent symbol. God is described in Exodus as a 'pillar of fire'. Fire is a symbol of creativity and energy, of the power of both destruction and creation. Wind and fire. Put the two together and we have symbols which denote enormous energy, considerable mystery, and great power. And so the followers of Jesus used the symbols of wind and fire as they tried to put into words their experience on the day of Pentecost. This is how the Book of Acts puts it:

The day of Pentecost had come, and they were all together in one place. Suddenly there came from the sky what sounded like a strong, driving wind, a noise which filled the whole house where they were sitting. And there appeared to them flames like tongues of fire distributed among them, and coming to rest on each one. They were all filled with the Holy

Spirit and began to talk in other tongues, as the Spirit gave them power of utterance (Acts 2.1–3).

There is something else to notice in that passage, and that is the significance of language. It goes on to say that a crowd . . . gathered, and were bewildered because each heard his own language spoken. What on earth could that mean? In common with much New Testament material, it is in part a reference back to the Old Testament, the Hebrew Bible. In Genesis 11 there is the fascinating story of the Tower of Babel. In part it is one of those marvellous stories in the early part of Genesis which purport to show how something strange or inexplicable came to be. There are several of these 'Just So' stories in that part of the Bible, and this is one of them. The technical name for such a story is an aetiological myth – a tale that is meant to explain something otherwise inexplicable. The puzzle behind the Babel story is, why do people speak so many different languages? We all belong to the human race. Why do we not speak the same language? Well, as in the cases of other stories of this kind, the Tower of Babel doesn't so much explain the puzzle as to acccommodate the puzzle into a framework that everyone would know.

But there is more to it than that. Wrapped up within the story is a Jewish suspicion that the huge towers they had become accustomed to in the land of Babylon (where the Babel story was probably constructed) were a sign of impiety and human pride. So the Tower of Babel was also a story about ways in which pride led to the disruption of human communities and, as a result, the discomforting of people by causing them to speak different languages. Some of us might reflect on that on our summer holidays, if we are south of Calais and the going gets difficult.

Please notice the use made of the Babel story in Acts 2. The remarkable thing about language on the day of Pentecost was that the early confusion of language was suddenly overcome. Foreigners could be understood. If the Tower of Babel marked the beginning of confusion and disunity among people,

Pentecost marked the beginning of a restored harmony and understanding. That is the symbolism which lies behind this part of the story of the day of Pentecost. The confusion and disunity of Babel was turned around by the coming of the Holy Spirit upon the disciples. Speaking unintelligibly was not the sign of God's presence: it is intelligible speech, a common understanding among people and the creation of inclusive communities, which is the gift of the Spirit.

On the day of Pentecost there were the symbols of wind and fire, and language was used to form a community of common understanding. There was also the impact of the Spirit on people's lives. How are we to understand that?

John V. Taylor, in a book first published in 1972, spoke of the Holy Spirit as the 'go-between'. 'We can never be directly aware of the Spirit, since in every experience of meeting and recognition, he is the go-between who creates awareness.'[2] He illustrates that in a moving re-telling of the story of the love of Dante for Beatrice. Dante, the great poet of renaissance Florence, was only nine years old when he first met Beatrice, who was just a few months younger. In spite of their tender age, she made a stupendous impression upon him. He remembered their first meeting with the visual clarity that sometimes accompanies a moment of special significance, and lingers ever after in the memory. When he saw her he remembered that his heart trembled, and he said: 'Behold, a god stronger than I that is come to bear rule over me'. Only occasionally after that did he see her, but it was not until she was eighteen that she first spoke to him. Later, at a party, she joined the other girls in making fun of him because he was so overwhelmed by his feelings for her. At twenty-one she married, and three years later she died. John Taylor commented:

That slender handful of brief encounters was fraught with stupendous power – power enough not only for the orientation of his own life, power not only to stamp his vision upon the whole of Western thought, but, as he claimed, cosmic power itself.[3]

He suggests that the final lines of the Divine Comedy were informed by that overpowering youthful experience:

Already my heart and will were wheeled by love,
The Love that moves the sun and the other stars.[4]

and he sees in this example the signs of the Spirit's activity: 'the creation of greater sensitivity, the compulsion to choose, and the call to sacrifice'.[5]

Human love can be cheap and trivial. But it can also be wonderful, immensely moving, and totally transforming. So can divine love. The Holy Spirit is what awakens us to ourselves and to others. What stirs within us the movement of great love, or an awareness of beauty, or a longing for truth, or the kind of energy which once could only be described by the symbols of a powerful tearing wind and a fire that seemed to burn in those who knew the Spirit.

How do you describe the indescribable? The people who started the church in motion on a day of Pentecost in Jerusalem used symbols, picture language, to convey what they could not describe. For us, the most effective symbols may be human love, a boy and a girl in renaissance Florence, or modern London or Paris. If the symbols are helpful they will convey the sense of wonder, of awakening, of a Spirit in ourselves that impels us towards the Spirit that moves the universe. And for us, too, the activity of the Spirit may be seen in an increase of awareness and sensitivity, of a deeper love and a greater joy, of creative communities which exist to serve others.

7 Why Seek the Living among the Dead?

The heroes of the story of the resurrection are the women. There is a strong – and surely a deliberate – contrast between the portrayal of the women and the men in the accounts of the resurrection experiences. The contrast is especially noticeable when the role of the women during the last days of the life of Jesus is compared with the story of Peter. Peter, remember, was the leading figure of the Jerusalem church. He came to be thought of later as the prototype of all future Christian leadership, and the first pope. Yet in the accounts of the trial, crucifixion and resurrection of Jesus, Peter is portrayed in a much less complimentary light than the women. In chapter 22 Luke tells of Peter following Jesus at a discreet distance to the high priest's house, after the arrest. He sat surreptitiously in the courtyard. A serving maid who saw him sitting in the firelight stared at him, and said: 'This man was with him too.' But Peter denied it. 'I do not know him,' he said. A little later a man sitting there said, 'You are also one of them.' Peter was emphatic. 'No, I am not.' An hour later someone else connected Peter's accent with the Galilean followers of Jesus. 'Of course he was with them. He must have been; he is a Galilean. But Peter said, "I do not know what you are talking about" ' (Luke 22.54–60). So the story of Peter's loss of courage is played out.

By contrast notice what is written about the women. When, after many indignities, Jesus was led away to execution it was said that 'great numbers of people followed, among them many women who mourned and lamented over him' (Luke 23.49). They remained throughout the crucifixion, standing with 'his

friends' and watching it all. Afterwards, it was the women who
followed Joseph of Arimathaea when he took the body, and
they remembered the location of the tomb where the body was
laid. Then they went home, prepared spices and perfumes, and
rested on the sabbath day before returning to the tomb 'very
early on the first day of the week' (Luke 24.1).

After the arrest, mention of the male disciples is tentative.
They remain at a distance, almost like a military leader who
urges troops on into danger and death with the cry, 'forward
into battle, chaps; I'm well behind you'. But there is no
mention of women running away, or of concealing their
identity. They had followed all the way from Galilee, and they
were there to the end. And very early on the first Easter Day, it
was the women, not the men, who came to the tomb.

In the light of that, the words which according to Luke were
addressed to the women by the guardian of the tomb – 'Why
do you seek the living among the dead? He is not here, but has
risen' (Luke 24.5 RSV) – provide a suitable basis for an Easter
reflection. The resurrection, the story of Easter, is about a kind
of revolution. It describes a reversal of normally accepted
values, and a turning upside-down of our expectations. The
way the women are incorporated into the story makes the
revolutionary nature of it very clear. It was not entirely new,
of course, because the ministry of Jesus had all along been
marked by an unconventional attitude towards women. But the
resurrection narrative uses what, for the time, was an unusual
relationship between a religious leader and women to bring out
the reversal of values which is central to the Easter message.

Jesus is pictured in the Gospels as having been unusually
relaxed in his dealings with women. He spoke to strange women
in public, against the conventions of the time. When John's
Gospel tells of him speaking to a Samaritan woman alone by a
well, it also adds: 'His disciples returned, and were astonished
to find him talking with a woman' (John 4.27). Against
convention, it is said that Jesus touched women and ate with
them, and those women included some shady characters,
including probably a prostitute. He even taught women, as

though they could become his pupils or disciples, a practice that again was contrary to the accepted ideas of the time. In the story of Mary and Martha, Martha's complaint was not only that she had all the chores to do; it was also that Mary was sitting at the feet of Jesus, listening to his teaching and discussing it with him, and so adopting a male, not a female, role (Luke 10.38–42). His treatment of women was unconventional; probably unconventional enough to arouse suspicions and prompt snide comments among some of those who saw him. In Luke 13 there is a story of a woman who had been 'bent double' with some kind of spinal disease for eighteen years. In the eyes of many, she suffered from two disabilities; she was a woman, and as a diseased woman she was possessed by Satan. In the ensuing controversy about healing on the sabbath, Jesus referred to her as 'a daughter of Abraham' (a phrase rarely if ever found in Jewish literature of the time). It implied that she was to be regarded as a fully-fledged member of the Covenant community, of equal standing before God with men (Luke 13.10–17).

In the roles attributed to women in the resurrection narratives, the Gospels show a reversal of the commonly accepted values of the time. In that way they suggest that our expectations are turned upside down by the happenings described as 'resurrection'. The events are revolutionary.

But what was the experience the women had? They found the tomb empty, and the text says that as they stood amazed at not being able to find the body of Jesus 'two men in dazzling garments were at their side'. What are we to make of that? The two men are often depicted as angels. I am never very confident about angels. We use them poetically, as in angel voices ever singing. Or more strikingly, in the Christmas carol 'Once in royal David's city', with its final lines conjuring up visions of angelic little children:

> When like stars his children crowned
> All in white shall stand around.[1]

Is it deliberate bathos? Given the nineteenth-century date and the author, probably not. I suppose if we were to put two parts of our national heritage together, those lines might provide us with a mental picture of small boys in some wretched prep school being bored to death on a cricket field.

'What do you do on summer afternoons?'
'Oh, we dress up in white and stand around.'
'You mean you play cricket?'
'Yes, something like that.'

I don't think I want to stand around, whether dressed in white or some other colour. Indeed, I suppose the fear of many of us as we grow older is that we might spend our last years standing around. We surely don't want to do it after death as well. So I worry about angels.

But I suspect that is not a necessary worry here. Even a conservative biblical scholar, Howard Marshall, says of this part of Luke 24: 'the angelic message . . . is a literary device to bring out the significance of the discovery'.[2] There, a literary device. That's better, even if the device doesn't work very well for us today. It is meant to heighten the sense of astonishment and wonder that the body of Jesus had not been found. The main emphasis here is on the experience of the women, who were said to be 'terrified' and 'filled with fear'. That we can understand better. Fear and awe and wonder are all elemental religious feelings. They suggest a sense of something a little beyond our grasp that might be powerful, and even threatening to the even tenor of our lives. The women's experience was a genuine religious experience. Not only were they capable of receiving religious teaching (a male prerogative); not only were they able to follow a teacher around the country (a male prerogative); they were also the ones who first had that powerful, moving and terrifying experience which was at the heart of what 'resurrection' means. With that sense of fear and awe upon them, the women went to tell the apostles. 'The story appeared to them to be nonsense, and they would not believe it.'

That was sad, in the context. But to how many people today

does the Easter story appear to be nonsense? If we don't want it to be nonsense for us, let's go back to the experience of the women, and especially to the question in Luke 24. 'Why do you seek the living among the dead?' The tomb was not the place to look. Not then. Not now. Out in the world is where Christians are called to live the resurrection life. Looking in the tomb; worrying about whether it happened just as the Gospel texts have it; saying the words of the creed: 'I believe in the resurrection of the body'; that doesn't help. Anybody can say that. Anyone can read the text. Why search for the living among the dead?

What the resurrection might be about for us is rather different. It is about something much more radical, much more urgent, much more exciting, much more liberating. The tomb is not the place to look. The resurrection is still to be found in experience. An experience of things turning upside down, a reversal of normally accepted values, a change of expectation, a revolutionary message.

The resurrection is not to be found by espousing the values and qualities which most people think drive the world: toughness, aggression, dominance, hierarchical rule, violence – the qualities we often find stereotyped as 'masculine' qualities (we understand of course that women as well as men can allow themselves to be dominated by those 'masculine' qualities, just as men as well as women can possess 'feminine' qualities). The revolutionary message of the resurrection, however, suggests that what are thought to be feminine qualites are the ones to be espoused – sensitivity to the powerless; compassion; gentleness; love; non-violence; and co-operation rather than domination. In the texts of the Gospels, that is where resurrection life is to be found.

8 Why Did Jesus Die?

'Jesus died for you' says the convinced evangelical Christian. The Christian Union, currently the most popular of Christian student organizations, goes further. Its doctrinal basis, required to be signed by all who join, sets out eleven 'fundamental truths of Christianity' among which is belief in 'redemption from the guilt, penalty and power of sin, only through the sacrificial death once and for all time of our representative and substitute, Jesus Christ, the only mediator between God and man'. Evidently the message is not only 'Jesus died for you' but 'Jesus died to take away the guilt, penalty and power of sin' from you and me. I find that idea astonishingly opaque. It sounds so mechanical, as though something is done for us almost magically, without our being in any way involved. I can grasp the concept of, say, a friend putting himself between me and an assassin, and so dying in my place. That would be an act of heroism, and would also have 'saved' me. But how can a death nearly two thousand years ago in another part of the world have been intended to relate directly to me? It sounds a very strange idea. Yet the atonement, the doctrine that the death of Jesus Christ avails for those who believe in him, appears to be central to Christianity. What are we to make of it?

First, let's notice that there are many ideas of the atonement. The interpretation of the doctrine quoted above is by no means the only one. Even the most devout Christian is not necessarily tied to that. Secondly, we have to recognize that ideas about the atonement have often been conditioned by cultural, social and even political structures. That is one reason why some of them now seem so remote. They no longer fit with ways we think about our world.

Some early views of the atonement related to worship that took place in the temple in Jerusalem during the lifetime of Jesus. In John's Gospel, Jesus is hailed as 'the Lamb of God who takes away the sin of the world' (John 1.29). The 'lamb' is a reference to Jewish sacrificial practice, and Jesus is there being presented as somehow replacing temple sacrifice. Does that mean that Jesus becomes the sacrifice, or simply that sacrificial conduct, behaviour befitting a follower of Jesus, replaces ritual worship? In any case, we must recognize that in John's Gospel 'sin' is characteristically a failure to recognize or to believe in the revelation of the *logos*, the truth, in Jesus. Sin is ignorance of that truth, rather than wilful misbehaviour. In that context, Jesus 'takes away' the sin of the world by revealing the truth.[1]

The death of Jesus has also been seen as a ransom paid to the devil, who has the world in thrall and needs a bribe if he is to set it free. It has been related to ideas of divine justice, with the suggestion that in justice God could not forgive people's sins without receiving some satisfaction in return.[2] It has been understood as the reversal of the sin of Adam. And so on. What are we to make of it all? Are the ideas not remote and mechanical? Do they have anything directly to do with us, or with the death of Jesus?

Even in times long past, Christians have not always held to such ideas. Peter Abelard, a radical thinker of the eleventh and twelfth centuries, rejected them all. He argued that if God wanted to forgive people's sins, he could do so, pointing out that Jesus offered forgiveness to Mary, and to the paralysed man, without first suffering anguish on the cross. It was the example of Jesus that mattered to Abelard, who believed that '. . . by the life and death of His Son He has so bound us to Himself that love so kindled will shrink from nothing for his sake. Our redemption is that supreme devotion kindled in us by the Passion of Christ'.[3] That echo from centuries ago may be a little more in keeping with the way we are likely to think about such things now.

So why did Jesus die?

First, and most simply, we have to acknowledge that Jesus

died because of the Roman authorities. They ruled Palestine in what for them were difficult times. Jewish nationalists were anxious to wrest control of their country from Roman hands. During the lifetime of Jesus there were guerrilla movements, reprisals, the beginnings of an uprising, and many of the features of people struggling against colonial rule which have been so familiar this century. Whether by design or not, Jesus was caught up in those movements. When the Romans executed him they nailed to his cross what they regarded as the basis for the charge against him. They believed he had claimed or was thought to be: 'The King of the Jews' (Mark 15.26). That may have been a misunderstanding of the real motives that drove Jesus, but it was not entirely without foundation. Among the closest disciples of Jesus were two men who may have been associated with revolutionary movements: there was Simon the Canaanaean, a term more probably derived from the Aramaic for Zealot than from the village of Cana; and there was Judas Iscariot, whose second name may have been a corruption of Sicarii, or 'dagger man'.[4]

In the minds of the Roman authorities, who condemned him and carried out the execution, the death of Jesus had to do with fears of rebellion.

Secondly, Jesus died because he had adopted for himself the role of the suffering servant prefigured in Isaiah. The prophet had spoken movingly about the figure of a servant, who would accept suffering rather than cause it:

> He will not shout or raise his voice,
>   or make himself be heard in the street.
> He will not break a crushed reed
>   or snuff out a smouldering wick;
> Unfailingly he will establish justice (Isa. 42.2–3).

Isaiah might have been speaking of the whole nation of Israel as his servant; certainly, the words could have been applied to the people of Israel at many different stages of their history. Or he might have been referring to a minority within the nation, who held on to their religious and moral values, and to their

Jewish identity, in times of adversity. Or he might have had in mind a single individual, whose witness was peaceful, whose concern was justice, and whose destiny was suffering and death. Whatever or whoever it was the prophet had in mind, it is natural enough that Christians should have applied the words to Jesus, as one who was 'pierced for our transgressions, crushed for our iniquities . . . the Lord laid on him the guilt of us all' (Isa. 53.5, 6).

From the time of his temptations, when alternative patterns of behaviour to do with the use of political power, the exploitation of economic gifts, or the use of near-magical powers where all rejected, Jesus was left with one outstanding biblically-inspired alternative in the poignant but powerful image of the suffering servant. Refusing to exploit the support of the crowds on Palm Sunday, Jesus almost inevitably found himself caught up in the agony of the Garden of Gethsemene. 'Maltreated' and 'submissive . . . he was cut off from the world of the living' (Isa. 53.7, 8). The suffering servant was one who refused to take up the weapons of violence, and so had to be willing to bear violence in his own person. Obedience to that particular vision encouraged Jesus in his acceptance of death.

Why did Jesus die? Thirdly, he died because he acted with complete selflessness. This was both his most special quality and a reason for his death. Jesus is described in the New Testament as one who 'laid no claim to equality with God, but made himself nothing, assuming the form of a slave. Bearing the human likeness, sharing the human lot, he humbled himself, and was obedient even to the point of death, death on a cross!' (Phil. 2.7f.).

Having rid himself of all self-seeking, and having opposed the 'principalities and powers' of his time and place, Jesus had willingly exposed himself to the danger of those who eschew the weapons of their opponents and lay claim instead to the weapons of persuasion, love and self-sacrifice. The young German theologian, Dietrich Bonhoeffer, who himself became a martyr for his Christian faith and convictions in his opposition to the Nazis in the Second World War, suggested that it was the complete self-emptying of Jesus that formed the basis of his claim to divinity.[5] In a lecture on Bonhoeffer to mark the fiftieth anniversary of his death, Keith Clements recalled the record of a conversation between Bonhoeffer, his brother-in-law, Hans Von Dohnyani, and other conspirators against the Nazis. Bonhoeffer quoted the words of Jesus from Matthew's Gospel, 'all they that take the sword shall perish with the sword'. Dohnyani, a lawyer and a leading figure in the anti-Nazi movement asked, 'does that mean us also?' 'Yes', Bonhoeffer replied, 'it does.'[6] Those who were willing to stand against tyranny in Nazi Germany had to count the cost, and be prepared to pay. A willingness to sacrifice, to stand powerless against overwhelming odds armed only with conviction, truth and justice, was demanded of those who attempted to follow Jesus Christ in that dire situation of war. It reflected the self-giving of Jesus, who is for Christian people the supreme example of the great love of God, revealed much less in acts of power and might than in selfless giving; in standing unarmed save for truth and integrity against the principalities and powers of this world.

Jesus died because to the Roman authorities he appeared a threat and a possible symbol around which rebellion might have gathered.

He died because he had rejected a number of feasible models of a messiah figure in favour of the suffering servant sketched by the prophet Isaiah.

He died chiefly in a great demonstration of the limitless love of God, which is not the sentimental stuff of modern romances, but a self-giving for the sake of others which stands against oppression and violence and greed and fear. It is that self-giving which most clearly characterizes Jesus; and that is a quality which even ordinary, timid Christian people can on occasion emulate and make their own.

9 On Not Clinging to Jesus

We all cling to things. The baby clings to its mother; the young child to a comforter or a thumb; children to the security of a home; teenagers to the bewilderment of a disappearing childhood or to a peer group; adults to their fading youth, to a job, or status, or reputation. We all cling to something. One of life's hard lessons, however, is that while we may cling to things by nature, we have to learn to let go by our own volition. Students sometimes bring their teddy bears with them to university; but the middle-aged man who insisted on taking a worn piece of blanket – his childhood comforter – to bed with him would arouse at best suspicion and at worst a fair degree of derision. We all cling. And we all have to learn to let go.

Is it possible that such an idea is implied in words said to have been spoken by Jesus to Mary, outside the empty tomb? 'Do not cling to me, said Jesus, for I have not yet ascended to my Father and your Father, to my God and your God' (John 20.17).

So should we not even cling to Jesus? Doesn't that sound preposterous? Christian hymns, even some of the great ones, use images which clearly convey the sense of clinging to Jesus. It was Charles Welsey who wrote:

Never let me leave thy breast,
From thee, my Saviour stray.[1]

That was in the context of a hymn in which it is clear that the language is symbolic. The same may not be said so readily of some modern songs and choruses.

Are we not supposed to cling to Jesus? Yet here are words attributed to Jesus himself, saying 'Do not cling to me'. And in a passage often read in connection with the ascension, there are also the words: 'It is in your interests that I am leaving you' (John 16.7). The ascension is not much referred to publicly these days, although it remains theoretically an important Christian festival. To people with no background in theology, it must sound odd indeed. Even those of us who are within the tradition may find it harder to interpret than most festivals. Many of the hymns and biblical passages associated with the ascension sound to modern ears like a story of an astronaut. There is little doubt that many Christians used to take such references literally, as though Jesus did disappear into the sky as the disciples gazed towards the heavens. If you are like me, you will no longer be able to think about the ascension in that way.

The connection between the two verses from John's Gospel provides a clue to one way in which the Ascension may be interpreted. In John 20, in words addressed to Mary outside the empty tomb, and in John 16, in words addressed to the disciples in a long farewell discourse before the crucifixion, Jesus speaks about his departure. 'Do not cling to me for I have not yet ascended to the Father;' and 'Nevertheless I assure you that it is in your interest that I am leaving you.' Jesus is telling his followers that they will have to come to terms with living without his physical presence. As Kingsley Barrett remarked in his Commentary on John: 'The resurrection has made possible a new and more intimate spiritual union between Jesus and his disciples; the old physical contacts are no longer appropriate . . .'[2]

One aspect of the ascension that is clear is that it marked the beginning of a new phase. The disciples had followed Jesus, in some doubt but also with great enthusiasm and high expectations. Then came the dreadful time of the crucifixion, and the apparent dashing of their hopes. In ways that are to us inexplicable the resurrection convinced the disciples that what Jesus had said and done was still a living force among them; that the revelation of God encountered in him was as available – indeed, even more available – than it had been before. Still to come was their experience of the Holy Spirit, of the immanence of God within them and their community. In that intermediate period came the ascension – the clear awareness of the disciples, in the light of some of the words Jesus had said to them during his lifetime, that they would have to live without his physical presence. Now they had to take up the tasks he had committed to them. The words of St Teresa of Avila on this subject are well-known, but they will bear repetition.

> Christ has no body now on earth but yours, no hands but yours, no feet but yours; yours are the eyes through which to look out Christ's compassion to the world, yours are the feet with which he is to go about doing good, and yours are the hands with which he is to bless us now.

Jesus has departed. His unfinished work now has to be done through those who owe him allegiance, and attempt to follow and serve him in their own place and time. It is a startling thought that we should be regarded as Christ's representatives, his body, hands and feet. Not only does Christian faith have to be worked out in the experience of life to have meaning: Jesus Christ himself has to be represented by his followers. How may that be done? Jesus said to one of his disciples: 'Do not cling to me.' Don't spend all your time looking back on the past two or three years, however momentous they may have been. Remember them, cherish them, but be ready to move on so that you may be my servant in the world in which you will have to live.

It is not easy to do. All sorts of obstacles appear in our way. There is a strong temptation among Christians, as among people of all religious faith, to cling to the past. We are tempted to believe that the way people thought and acted in a desert community in the time of Moses, in the first century, at the time of the Reformation in the sixteenth century, or in the eighteenth-century experience of the Wesleys can be simply recreated at the end of the twentieth century. Our churches set up working parties to wrestle with great questions of our time – nuclear weapons, human sexuality, relations with people of other faith – and always there will be somebody who will say, 'but what about that verse in Leviticus?', or 'what did John Wesley think about that?'

We do it frequently when we cling to Jesus. There is a strong temptation to cling to the literal interpretation of a few carefully chosen texts, or doctrines, and to regard those as essential for our Christian life. It might have to do with a theory of the atonement. It might have to do with an inter-pretation of the birth stories or of the resurrection: believe in the virgin birth, and you will be saved; or believe in the physical metamorphosis of a body, and you will be saved. Put like that, the absurdity is immediately apparent, as is the con-trast with the teaching of Jesus. Jesus, we recall, did not always cling to current interpretations of Jewish law or tradition (although he took them seriously). He was more concerned to prod people into thinking about what the tradition or the texts might mean for them in their own times and their own situa-tion. No doubt it was a very provocative thing to do. 'You have heard that they were told, "Love your neighbour . . ."' But what about your enemies? How will you deal with them? Could you 'Love your enemies and pray for your persecutors'? (Matt. 5.43, 44). We have to remind ourselves that words can be idols. It is not only statues, images, or pictures which constitute idols; words can be idols, too. Words can become subsititutes for thinking about the implications of the teaching of Jesus; texts can become substitutes for an encounter with God himself. If we wish to avoid idolatry, we must pass beyond the idol, beyond the image or the text itself, to discover what it is meant to convey.[3]

'Do not cling to me,' said Jesus. For people in the churches today, clinging to Jesus often has to do with holding on to things that have passed: with forms of respectablity which belong to an earlier generation; with a rigidity of thinking which refuses to entertain new ideas; with a refusal to look with fresh eyes at old texts; with an unwillingness to accept that all institutions are inevitably growing and changing, and must adapt to new patterns. 'Back to basics' was an unfortunate political slogan; it is equally poor in religious terms. Being a Christian does not mean going into reverse in search of some imagined golden age; it means following, moving on to new challenges and more comprehensive thoughts. It means growing and developing in spirituality, and intellectual understanding, and service.

'Do not cling to me,' Jesus said to Mary. Be my follower still, but in the light of my teaching and my example and guided by the Spirit of God, work out your faith in the world in which you have to live. 'Do not cling to me' – to the physical Jesus of Nazareth – because new things will happen. And so it was. Christians were impelled to move on. Enthused by the Spirit, bound together into the community of the church; living by the grace and the love of God; and called to communicate that love and grace to others, Christians had to move on and relate their faith to new places and different times, to issues not known before and to cultural and social contexts widely different from those of first century Palestine. The Christian community and Christian people are always having to learn how to get along without Jesus, without his voice, his hands, and his presence in the world.

Many of us know to our cost how difficult and painful it can be to get along without somebody. We know pain in bereavements which gives rise to the constant desire to call back and re-live days that have gone. I remember in the early 1980s interviewing a considerable number of people then active in the civil rights movement in the United States. One of the things that surprised me was the frequent criticism I heard of Coretta King, widow of Martin Luther King Jr. The civil rights people knew that they had to move on. Much as they had admired Martin Luther King, they knew that they could not stop where he had been stopped so cruelly. They had to go on beyond 1968, and deal with new issues, just as Martin would have done had he lived. They felt that his widow had become stuck in a kind of museum, that she was making a mausoleum of his memory instead of travelling on with them. They were not saying, 'Let her forget him.' They were saying, 'In remembering and honouring his memory, she must stop clinging to the past and move on to what Martin would be doing now.'

That is part of the meaning of the ascension. As Christians we cannot cling to the past, however unique and formative it may have been for us. Together, in each generation, we have to work out what it means to live the Gospel. 'Do not cling to me,' says Jesus. As his people in the world of our own day, we have to learn how to be his servants, how to do his work, how to represent Christ in our communities.

10 Salvation

'Brother, are you saved?' Perhaps there are Christians who still greet people with such words. The most likely response will be an embarrassed silence. But some might say 'yes'; braver souls might say 'no'; and the difficult – or thoughtful – ones among us might say, 'It depends what you mean by saved.'

What is meant by the question? A common perception is that Christians are obsessed with an idea of salvation which relates to an unknowable future, to heaven or hell. Many critics appear to assume that going to church or engaging in church-related activities must necessarily be for the perverted reason of gaining a heavenly reward. And there may be something in that. Among the baggage we inherit is the attitude that if we behave ourselves (according to some religious prescription, no doubt); if we submit to churchly rites and routines; if we say that we believe the 'right' things, then although we may not have a great time here we shall be recompensed hereafter.

But if such assumptions are compared with biblical material some surprises emerge. In English translations of the Old Testament there are a number of Hebrew words translated as 'salvation'. The commonest of them is the word *yasha*, which means to be delivered, or helped, or to have victory in battle. The root meaning of it is to be broad, to enlarge, to be spacious. Now I suppose asking somebody 'Brother, are you saved?' has rather different connotations from saying, 'Sister, are you broad, have you grown spacious?' But it is from such a beginning that the word came to mean deliverance, liberation, and then salvation. And if we think about it in context, then it immediately becomes clear that 'deliverance' in the Hebrew

Bible has a very practical meaning. In the stories of Moses and the Exodus from Egypt, salvation was quite specifically deliverance from slavery and into the freedom of an independent people. That is why the story of the Exodus has been echoed so strongly in liberation theology and in the preaching of churches such as those living under apartheid in South Africa. 'Let my people go' is a splendid text for preachers with a social conscience in places where people live under oppressive regimes. And in the continuing traditions of Judaism, little has been made of what Christians often mean by 'salvation'; but the concepts of deliverance, liberation, and being free in the land have continued to be very important. That is clear enough.

What may be more surprising is that New Testament references to salvation also tend to be quite practical. The common word [*soteria*] means preservation and safety, as well as salvation. In Acts 7 there is a long speech by Stephen, who is reminding a Jewish Council of their common history as it is set out in the Bible. He refers to the story of Moses, and of how Moses went to the help of one of his fellow Jews who was being ill-treated by an Egyptian. The text says that Moses 'thought his countrymen would understand that God was offering them deliverance through him . . .' The word translated 'deliverance' is *soterian*. In Hebrews 11 it is said that 'by faith Noah . . . built an ark to save his household'. The word is the same, *soterian*. The sense in those passages is still clearly that of rescue or deliverance from a dangerous situation.

There are very few references to salvation in the Gospels. It was not a word much upon the lips of Jesus. There is that reference at the end of Mark's Gospel, which says: 'Afterwards, Jesus sent out by them, from east to west, the imperishable message of eternal salvation' (Mark 16.8b). That is how it is in the English translation: the problem with it is that the words do not appear in the best Greek texts, and it is widely regarded as a late addition, with the original ending of the Gospel occurring in the preceding sentence. Morna Hooker regards it as having been 'written by someone familiar with Hellenistic thought'.[1] Salvation, in those terms, is not natural to either the old

Testament or the Gospels. It's more natural to Greek thought. There's a discovery!

Yet are there not some references to salvation in Luke? Certainly. Most of them are found in the first chapter, which provides a transition between the Old Testament and the Gospels. The word for 'salvation' in Luke 1 is very similar in meaning to what is found in Exodus and elsewhere in the Hebrew Bible. Indeed, the word is twice translated 'deliver' (Luke 1.69, 71), and even in verse 77, where it is said that God will 'lead his people to a knowledge of salvation' the sense is very much of practical, indeed political, deliverance. Although the word itself does not appear there, it is a similar idea of salvation which appears in that other great song in Luke 1, the Song of Mary, also known as the Magnificat. Perhaps it doesn't seem to fit very well with particularly English interpretations of Christianity, bound up as they are with the sovereign as head of the Church in England, but members of the royal family, like other Anglicans, regularly repeat such words as:

> He has shown the might of his arm, he has routed the proud and all their schemes; he has brought down monarchs from their thrones, and raised on high the lowly. He has filled the hungry with good things and sent the rich empty away (Luke 1.51–53).

The word for salvation does admittedly appear more frequently in the Letters of the New Testament than in the Gospels. Sometimes there it assumes the sense that was also found in the Greek mystery religions. That is, of salvation taking a person out of this world into some other place, there to enjoy a reward. But this does not appear to be the common understanding of the Gospels. And it is only sometimes that such a meaning is found in the Letters.

Elsewhere in the New Testament, the verb 'to be saved' often means deliverance from disease. Think for a moment of that often-quoted verse from Acts 4 – for many Christians, an argument-clincher on the subject of salvation. Peter, leader of the Jerusalem church, is speaking to Jewish rulers, elders and scribes following the healing of a lame man. Peter says of Jesus, 'There is no salvation through anyone else; in all the world no other name has been granted to mankind by which we can be saved.'

It's regarded as a proof text. So what does it prove? Salvation here can hardly have to do with matters of eternal destiny. What Peter is defending is the healing of a lame man who had been sitting by the Gate Beautiful in Jerusalem. It is to do with healing. It is very close to the Old Testament sense of salvation as deliverance from some immediate peril. The man has been healed in the name of Jesus. That is what his salvation was. Naturally enough, in the light of his experience, Peter says: 'There is no other name by which we can be saved' [healed]. Many years ago, when I worked in India, I was privileged to be part of a community of people in Vellore most of whom worked in the great Christian Medical College and Hospital. Many of them were devout Christians. They worked in that splendid Medical College and Hospital as an expression of a Christian vocation, and they used their highly developed and varied skills to heal people. In that sense, they healed 'in the name of Jesus'. They used their knowledge of medical sciences to do so, but their commitment and life-style and reason for doing the work they did was that it expressed for them what it was to follow Jesus. Their daily work had to do with practical matters of health and healing, not with people's eternal destiny. It was nevertheless healing (the New Testament would have said 'salvation' [soteria: healing or deliverance]) in the name of Jesus.

Acts 4.12 reflects an argument between different groups of Jews about healing. It would be odd to take from that verse the idea that nobody who follows a religion other than Christianity could be 'saved' in the sense of securing their eternal destiny.

In the New Testament, it is God who is the Saviour. Sometimes that means that he is our deliverer from political oppression or some imminent peril. Sometimes he delivers from disease. But in the New Testament, God is also described in many other ways. He is Father, Lord, Judge.[2] Are those descriptions more or less important than 'Saviour'? What is chiefly expressed in the Bible by words about salvation is consistent with those other terms. It has to do with a sense of God's faithfulness to those who turn to him. It has to do with the biblical picture of God as compassion and care, love and light, truth and justice. To isolate one element of that, as the traditional use of the phrase, 'Brother are you saved?' appears to do, seems to reflect a total misunderstanding of the Gospel message.

Then what of our particular Christian traditions, and hymn-books and familiar pieties? Surely the Wesleys were concerned to save people in the way I have suggested is of little interest in the Gospels? Well, perhaps they were. Some Wesleyan hymns are difficult to sing if you have no interest in the theory of blood-atonement. Charles Wesley's splendid 'conversion' hymn begins with the question:

And can it be that I should gain
An interest in the Saviour's blood?[3]

And it clearly expects the answer 'yes'. In the same section of the hymnbook, there is a hymn of the Moravian, Zinzendorf, translated by John Wesley, with the words:

Jesus, thy blood and righteousness
My beauty are, my glorious dress.

If you are like me, you may find it difficult to get into the mind of somebody who thinks like that. But wait! There is something else, something quite different in the same tradition. Charles Wesley's hymn which is based on the story of Jacob includes the lines:

Pure universal love thou art;
To me, to all, thy mercies move:
Thy nature and thy name are love.[4]

The Wesleys' chief message had to do with God's universal

love. It can be argued that John Wesley was not much interested
in doctrine. He was an experiential thinker, interested in practical matters and people's experience much more than in
theoretical philosophical or theological debates. He once wrote:
'. . .orthodoxy, or right opinion, is at best but a very slender
part of religion, if it can be allowed to be any part at all'.[5]
His aim, he said, 'was to promote, so far as I am able, vital,
practical religion; and by the grace of God to beget, preserve
and increase the life of God in the souls of men'.[6]

That brings us back to Jesus, and the message of the Gospels.
Jesus, of course, was a Jew, and although critical of many
aspects of contemporary Jewish practice, his teaching inevitably
reflects a number of important Jewish emphases. Judaism has
always been concerned with what also interested John Wesley;
that is, with 'practical religion'. It is much more concerned with
how to live day by day with neighbours and family, in political
and social life, than with grand metaphysical theories about a
life to come. The religion is expected to work and to provide
help here in this life. That was the tradition into which Jesus
was born, in which he grew up, and within which his teaching
took place. So it is no surprise that in the teaching of Jesus as
it is reflected in the Gospels that same emphasis on practical
religion was overwhelmingly present.

The teaching of Jesus constantly emphasized God as Father.
Call God *Abba*, Father, he said; and that implied that God's
concern and compassion reached out to everyone, and could be
replicated in their lives. Think of God as a God of forgiveness
and love, he said, in such stories as that of the Prodigal Son,
and then try to align yourselves with that divine mercy and
love. According to Luke, when Jesus was beginning his public
ministry he deliberately chose a passage from the prophet Isaiah
to provide him with a kind of manifesto:

> The Spirit of the Lord is upon me . . .
> he has sent me to announce good news to the poor,
>   to proclaim release for prisoners
>   and recovery of sight for the blind;

to let the broken victim go free,
to proclaim the year of the Lord's favour.[7]

It was in such practical matters of liberation and deliverance that Jesus himself recognized salvation.

11 What is Scripture?

In Salman Rushdie's celebrated and notorious book, *The Satanic Verses*, there is a story of a scribe who alters a text. Gibreel had a dream; and part of the dream was of a Persian scribe called Salman who wrote down the words given him by the prophet Mahound. One day Salman altered a verse ever so slightly. The prophet said 'all-hearing, all-knowing' and Salman wrote 'all-knowing, all-wise'. The odd thing was that the prophet didn't notice. So Salman deliberately made greater mistakes. Given a reference to 'Christian', he wrote 'Jew'. Surely the prophet couldn't miss that? But he did! The scribe left the tent with tears in his eyes. He had made the terrible discovery that even a text which purports to be revelation can be altered by human foible.[1]

That may have been one part of *The Satanic Verses* to which some Muslims took exception. It raises very sharply the question: What is scripture? Why and how is it different from other writing? Why does it demand special attention? At the end of readings from the Bible in church people often say, 'This is the word of the Lord'. And Christians refer to 'The Word of God in the Old Testament'. How are we to understand such phrases? We could make a start by looking at one Old Testament passage which has to do with the making of scripture. In the Book of Jeremiah it is said that: 'Jeremiah summoned Baruch son of Neriah, and Baruch wrote on the scroll at Jeremiah's dictation, everything the Lord had said to him' (Jer. 36.4).

Jeremiah believed he had a divine directive to commit to writing all his prophecies 'about Jerusalem, Judah, and all the nations' (Jer. 36.2). Baruch wrote down Jeremiah's words on a scroll, and then had the more dangerous job of reading the scroll to all the people. There was an immediate demand that Baruch should go and repeat his reading before the advisers and officials of the king. And that was followed by a reading of the words to the king himself by one of his own officials, Jehudi. The king took a knife, and as each section of the scroll was read he cut it off and threw it into the fire. That was his way of showing his contempt for the words of the prophet! Jeremiah was not to be silenced by the arrogance of a mere king. After all, he was declaring the words of God. So Jeremiah took another scroll, and Baruch took down the message all over again, this time with additions to the original.

The story is assumed to reflect in part the first stage in the writing of what was to become the Book of Jeremiah, which then became part of 'The Prophets', and in due course scripture for Jews and Christians alike.

Does that raise for us the question: How do words become scripture? Why do some sayings and writings become sacred texts? And what does it mean when they do?

When Jeremiah spoke his words to Baruch and they were written down, they were not scripture. They became that in the course of time. When Paul wrote his letters to Christian communities around the Mediterranean, his words were not scripture; they were advice and exhortation and teaching. They became scripture only in the course of time. When Jesus spoke to his disciples he spoke against a background of scripture, the background of the Hebrew Bible. Sometimes he treated it critically, and certainly he joined in debates about how passages should be interpreted. But the words of Jesus were not immediately scripture. They only became that in the course of time.

Scripture lives in communities, and it cannot be separated from them. The words of Jeremiah, the letters of Paul, the teaching of Jesus, all became scripture in the history of particular communities. It is people, and their communities, who make texts, or sayings, into scriptures and keep them that way.

A book by Wilfred Cantwell Smith contains a fascinating

example at some length of the use of one particular piece of scripture.[2] He writes about The Song of Songs. I wonder how many Christians read it today? Yet it was a favourite text in mediaeval times. There are more Latin manuscripts of The Song of Songs still in existence than of any other book. From only one of the four Gospels (John) and the Psalms were more sermons preached in that period. Is that surprising? John, the Psalms, and the Song of Songs as the most common sources of sermons. Preachers today might find that a considerable challenge. Rabbi Aqiba, who lived in the first or second century CE wrote: 'The whole of time is not worth the day on which The Song of Songs was given to Israel. All the writings are holy; The Song of Songs is the holy of holies.'[3]

Inevitably, there are different interpretations of The Song of Songs. In a Jewish interpretation it depicts the love of God for the Jewish community. The most popular Christian view is that it expresses Christ's love for the church, or for the soul of the individual member of the church. For mediaeval philosophers, the book expressed the love of God for the passive intellect.

Scriptures live in communities, and are part of the lives of the communities in which they develop, in which their limits are set and their authenticity proclaimed. Think for a moment of the biblical material which is also found in the Islamic scripture, the *Qur'an*. In the *Qur'an* we find the stories of the patriarchs, of Abraham, Moses and Jacob, common to Jews, Christians and Muslims alike. There are stories of Mary and Jesus, common to Christians and Muslims. But of course, the interpretation placed upon these stories differs with the different faiths.

For Jews, Abraham is the father of the Jewish people, whose significance lies in ways in which he foreshadowed the life of Israel, and settlement in the land. For Christians, Abraham is a model of faith, the man who 'obeyed the call to leave his home for a land which he was to receive as a possession; he went away without knowing where he was going' (Heb. 11.8). And for Muslims? In Islam, Abraham is honoured as the man who first received a revelation from God; the father, in that sense, of true faith and religion. Muslims believe that God gave his final revelation to Muhammad, who then had it recorded in Arabic in what became the *Qur'an*. They are consistent, therefore, in regarding their scripture as authentic only in Arabic. It may be translated for convenience, but the translation does not have the status of the Arabic text. If you want to read the *Qur'an* properly, you must first learn Arabic.

Christians have never taken that view of their scriptures. They have always been quite happy to use translations. It would be most unusual to sit in church and find your neighbour following the readings from Hebrew or Greek texts. At best, you might regard it as an affectation. Translations may only give an approximation of an original text, but for Christians the approximations have normally been regarded as good enough. Indeed the translation of scriptures into hundreds of languages has been regarded as a very important part of the mission of the church in the nineteenth and twentieth centuries.

We have also generally agreed as Christians that not all parts of the biblical texts are to be given the same value. Some parts are more important than others. Would even the most conservative of Christians in this country today agree to abide by the one ethical demand 'which is universal throughout the Old Testament and is expressed by lawgiver, prophet, psalmist and wise man, the total rejection of lending on interest' . . . ?[4]

Scriptures live and grow as part of the lives of communities; and they have to be interpreted. There is an interesting example of that in chapter seven of Mark's Gospel. The passage begins with a criticism of Jesus. 'Why do your disciples not conform to the ancient tradition, but eat their food with defiled hands?' (Mark 7.5) It appeared to his critics that the followers of Jesus were not paying proper attention to laws about ritual purity. The criticism was answered with a counter-attack. Jesus accused his critics of being obsessed with trivia, and he quoted the words of Isaiah against them: '. . . they teach as doctrines the commandments.of men'.[5] Taking the easy option of a literal interpretation, they had failed to think hard enough about what that part of the Torah meant. And he turned the argument by claiming that his critics were using the texts to support their own 'invented traditions' rather than to emphasize the intentions of the Torah. Is it not the case, he asked, that the commandment to 'honour your father and your mother' is deliberately evaded by those who dedicate their wealth to God in order to avoid supporting their parents? 'By your tradition, handed down among you, you make God's word null and void.' Consider what Torah intends, said Jesus. Don't try to evade the meaning of what is there in your scriptures. Then in verses 14 to 23, the same issue is rehearsed in a different way. Now Jesus appears to criticize the Levitical demands for purity, comparing commandments about ritual purity with those that have to do with moral purity. The contrast here is between two sections of the law, not between 'the commandments of God' and the 'commandments of men'.[6] Jesus both criticized and reinterpreted the tradition, as he often did. And we do it all the time. But that being so – and here is the crucial question – what is the basis for our reinterpretations, and our questioning, and our probing of scriptures?

May I go back for a moment to Muslims and the *Qur'an*? The *Qur'an*, I suggested, is regarded by the vast majority of Muslims as the unmediated word of God. The scripture *is* the revelation. It is not so for Christians. If modern fundamentalists claim that the Bible is in that sense the 'Word of God', they are mistaken in a dangerously deceptive way. For Christians, the Word of God, God's utterance, his revelation of himself, is contained in scripture, referred to in scripture, but is not scripture itself. In Christian understanding, God's self-disclosure, the utterance of his word, occurs in the natural world, in historical events, and through the words of his prophets. God 'speaks' in creation, through the message of the prophets, through the psalmists and the writers of the Wisdom books, but finally and supremely in the revelation that came with the birth, life, teaching, dying and rising again of Jesus Christ. Christ is God's revelation. Not a text. Scripture only bears witness to the revelation.

To Muslim friends we may say, there is your revelation in the *Qur'an*. We understand why you treat it with such reverence, handle it with loving care, and read it with awe and wonder. For you, it is the Word of God. But please do not compare it with the Bible. Our scriptures also live within a community. For Christians, they witness to the great event of Jesus Christ. But they are not synonymous with him.

For us, the revelation of God is seen supremely in the person of Jesus Christ, in whose light all scriptures, and all life, need to be understood.

Neighbours

12 Christianity – One Faith or Many?

I have a theory that the ecumenical movement began in 1910 and ended in 1972.[1] Let me explain what I mean by that.

Thirty years ago I was a presbyter of the Church of South India, working in the first and still one of the very few united churches to have incorporated both episcopal and non-episcopal traditions in one church. The Church of South India came into being in 1947, and brought together Anglicans, Methodists, Congregationalists, Church of Scotland and Reformed into one church. In the 1960s I was presbyter of St John's church, Vellore, where most of the congregation were simply 'Church of South India'. But in those days St John's had a very cosmopolitan congregation, including in its numbers people who had come from other areas of India and many parts of the world to work in the great Christian Medical College and Hospital in Vellore. In addition to those who had known no other tradition, there were Anglicans and Methodists from England and Australia, members of the Church of Scotland and of Congregational churches in Britain and the USA, American Baptists, Lutherans, and Reformed (sometimes confusingly called 'American Dutch Reformed'!), Swiss Evangelicals, and a substantial number from the Mar Thoma Church of Kerala, which traces its roots back to St Thomas. I have probably missed others represented there. But the congregation of St John's at that time represented a remarkable spectrum of Christian traditions, all happily gathered together into the life and worship of the Church of South India.

When I returned to England, it was to a united Methodist/United Reformed church on the borders of Kent and Sussex. Yet in spite of the achievement of that locally united church, in ecumenical terms it was like stepping back fifty years. St John's had been an Anglican church. Situated inside the well-preserved fourteenth-century fort at Vellore, for the first hundred years of its life it had been the garrison church for the British army in the area. In 1947 it experienced a double metamorphosis in becoming an Indian church and a united one. But attempting to explain to puzzled clergy of the diocese of Chichester that I had for the previous seven years been presbyter-in-charge of an ex-Anglican parish was to introduce a concept that was not so much odd as unthinkable.

The year was 1971. In 1972 the Anglican-Methodist proposals to form a united church failed. After that, ecumenical affairs in Britain took a different turn. There was a good deal of progress, of course. There was more friendly contact between people across a much wider spectrum. Catholics and Protestants were less inclined to believe of each other that they were virtually members of a different species; two-headed monsters, misbegotten in some dreadful doctrinal accident. The word was that unity was to grow from the grass-roots. And so it did. Ecumenical parishes were developed; united Free Churches were formed; but all on a local basis, while the denominations continued more or less in their old ways.

While that happened, other developments occurred. New Christian communities began to spring up – house churches, independent churches, charismatic groups – the one kind of Christian community (although of course it is not simply one kind) which has been growing in the past twenty years. Alongside that there has been a resurgence of – what can we call it? – let's say *conservative* Christian groups and people, sometimes fundamentalist, always quite close to that tendency, within as well as outside the mainline churches. That growth has challenged, and in so many ways overcome, the old liberal traditions which were once so strong in all the Free Churches, and indeed were common currency in the ecumenical movement until twenty years ago.

Hence the title. It has taken a long time, but here we are! Christianity – One Faith or Many? The modern ecumenical movement is widely regarded as having begun with a great conference at Edinburgh in 1910. It was a conference about cooperation in world mission, and it had as a slogan 'the conversion of the world in this generation'. The sentiments of the slogan never stood a chance of becoming reality. But out of that conference there grew the organizations that were to become the World Council of Churches. The medium became the message. Church leaders increasingly hoped for the formation of one great Christian body in which there could be brought together the scattered fragments of denominations. It was in 1972, or thereabouts, that the hope faded quietly away.

When I worked in the Church of South India my diocesan bishop was Lesslie Newbigin, a man of great gifts and integrity, and a church leader of outstanding quality. On the 27 September 1947, when the Church of South India came into being, Lesslie Newbigin became one of its first bishops. He later wrote about how moved he had been by the service at which the Church of South India was inaugurated.

> What has been done? Not, if we speak strictly, the inauguration of a 'Church' There can be but one Church. What has been done is that something which hid the true character of the Church has been repented of, and a very small step has been taken towards putting it away.[2]

It was a wonderful dream. Perhaps in some measure, some of it can yet be recovered. But in great sorrow we have to acknowledge that we shall not have any more churches on the model of the churches of South and North India. The ecumenical movement now is different. It is concerned much more with local initiatives than with great plans to unite denominations. Partly that is because the denominations are now very different. Today the differences between different kinds of Christians are no longer represented accurately by denominations. Within all denominations there are rifts between Christians who understand Christianity in fundamentally different ways. Denominations are less important. The kind of Christian faith people hold is much more important.

So is there one faith, or many? And in the midst of a plethora of different interpretations, how are we to find authentic Christian faith? The Gospels may help us there, because Jesus, a vigorous critic of much of the religious practice of his day, was involved on many occasions in controversy about what constituted faith; what was important in the tradition, and what was not.

An example of one such occasion is found in Matthew 12. In an enigmatic passage, questioners ask Jesus, 'Teacher, we would like you to show us a sign' (Matt. 12.38). It is a familiar religious request. All believers welcome some confirmation of their faith. But in response to that natural human desire, many fraudulent presentations of Christianity have arisen which in effect promise a sign, saying: 'If you will believe, you will have health, wealth, and happiness; things will go well with you.' Yet when we look at the picture of Jesus in the Gospels we see that his faith was maintained in spite of opposition and failure. It was maintained in the loneliness of the wilderness experience of the temptations; in the dereliction of the Garden of Gethsemene; in those places where no sign came, and faith had to be maintained in the face of silence. It is no surprise that when he was asked for a sign, he replied: 'It is a wicked, godless generation that asks for a sign, and the only sign that will be given it is the sign of the prophet Jonah.' Jesus himself is presented as God's sign. No other would be given.

To people who wanted reassurance and proof and certainty, as most people do, the message was that faith has to do with commitments that can only be verified after the event. Faith demands the following of the way of Jesus Christ, not because rewards are sprinkled along the path, enticing us onwards, but because of a belief that his way of sacrificial and loving care is in the end the right, indeed the only way.

One faith, or many? How do we recognize, and then respond to, authentic Christian faith? I began with a mention of Vellore, and the congregation there drawn mainly from the Christian Medical College and Hospital. One of the many remarkable pieces of work associated with CMCH is a Rural Unit for

Health and Social Affairs, which has attempted to pioneer new
ways of integrating medical treatment with social and economic
development in rural areas. The first Director of RUHSA was
a dynamic young doctor called Daleep Mukherjee. I recall a
meeting of the Trustees of RUHSA in this country at which Dr
Mukherjee was asked, 'What do you look for in students who
have been trained in Vellore? What difference should it make
that they have been at a *Christian* medical college?' His un-
hesitating answer was that such students should be motivated
more by a desire to offer service than to earn a large salary or
to gain high status.

That view of Christian vocation is echoed in stirring words
of Paul, writing to encourage a church in difficult circumstances. In a powerful and evocative passage, he wrote:

> We recommend ourselves by innocent behaviour and grasp
> of truth, by patience and kindness, by gifts of the Holy Spirit,
> by unaffected love, by declaring the truth, by the power of
> God. Honour and dishonour, praise and blame are alike our
> lot: we are the imposters who speak the truth, the unknown
> men whom all men know; dying we still live on; disciplined
> by suffering, we are not done to death; in our sorrows we
> have always cause for joy; poor ourselves, we bring wealth
> to many; penniless, we own the world (II Cor. 6.6–10).

Is that authentic Christianity? Years ago now, in 1982, I
visited what was then East Germany, and travelled to the far
south-eastern corner of the country to a small town called
Herrnhutt to deliver a lecture at a conference of European
Methodist Churches. After the conference I spent the weekend
in Leipzig, sharing in a local church conference and preaching
on the Sunday morning in the Kreuzkirche (the Church of the
Cross). Like many buildings in East Germany it had been rebuilt
with the bricks taken from the ruins of the previous church,
destroyed during the Second World War. It had been a difficult
country in which to be a Christian. There were some jobs open
only to those who were members of the Communist Party – and
you could not be a party member and a church member.

Christians were outsiders in that society. But the ones I met were enormously impressive people. Many of them were in the forefront of their country's powerful peace movement. They were firmly committed to what in their circumstances could not have been other than authentic Christian faith. Their experience had been a little like that of St Paul: '. . . disciplined by suffering, we are not done to death . . . poor ourselves, we bring wealth to many.'

There in Leipzig and Herrnhutt I saw a part of the world church that could give inspiration and hope to much more comfortable people elsewhere and provide insight into the strength and power of Christian faith in the modern world. There, among people refined by suffering and adversity, were signs of authentic Christianity. From India, from Germany and from many other parts of the world, we find inspiration and encouragement in lived examples of authentic Christianity.

Not in signs and promises, but in commitment and faith and hope do we find the authentic Christian faith of our day. Sadly, we shall no longer find signs of Christian faith in the organic unity of the churches that once we so longed for – perhaps that, too, for our generation, is a sign that is not granted, a fulfilment that is not to be. Instead, we have to struggle, in the midst of much spurious Christianity, for a gospel message which understands that no sign will be given to this generation except the sign of Jonah, the sign of Christ himself, who was despised and afflicted, and held to be of no account.

In the midst of churches torn by different interpretations and varied expectations, we have to hang on to a vision of authentic Christianity: ' . . . dying, we still live on; disciplined by suffering, we are not done to death; in our sorrows we have always cause for joy; poor ourselves, we bring wealth to many . . .'

So may it be.

13 The Decade of Evangelism in the Light of Several Decades of Dialogue

What do you expect of a decade of evangelism? The idea has been taken up by many Christians, and has been commended by archbishops and bishops as well as by other church leaders. Catholics have tended to speak of 'evangelization', which is taken to include those things often referred to as 'mission': not just preaching, but teaching, healing, education, health care and so on. Protestants have used the word 'evangelism', which suggests the proclamation of the gospel in words. Neither term is precisely biblical. What the New Testament refers to is the *euangelion*, the 'Good News', the gospel proclaimed in word and deed as Christians witness to their faith in Jesus Christ.

Few Christians would want to quarrel with the intention of proclaiming the gospel with particular vigour during this final decade of the millennium. But signals sent out by some enthusiasts have set alarm bells ringing. Dr Zaki Badawi, a moderate Muslim leader and chairman of the Imam's and Mosques Council, expressed his concern at what he feared might be an assault on Muslims in this country. In part that fear was aroused by an agency which originated in the USA but has since been sponsored by the Church of England, and was given the unfortunate name of Spearhead. Spearhead! To anyone with any sensitivity, the word recalls the shameful history of the Crusades – still a live issue in Muslim-Christian relationships. Dr Badawi said 'These plans for converting people of other faiths, made with Dr Carey's authority, add fuel to the disputes that divide society . . . Muslims are being whipped up into thinking there is another crusade.' Dr Carey replied that Spearhead is aimed at 'lapsed Christians and those indifferent to any faith'. But the suspicion remained. The Chief Rabbi, Jonathan Sacks, worried about the actions of a group dedicated to the conversion of Jews, said that the aggressive missionary activities of 'Jews for Jesus' shows 'disturbing insensitivity'.[1]

There appears to be a style of evangelism which imperils community relations. It is a style described in the New Testament as 'proselytizing', enticing someone from one faith to another. Jesus was very critical of that, saying to those who engaged in the practice: 'You travel over sea and land to win one convert; and when you have succeeded you make him twice as fit for hell as you are yourselves' (Matt. 23.15).

The first thing we need to notice as we think about evangelism and dialogue is that there is an important difference between the proclamation of the gospel and proselytizing. Proselytizing suggests a kind of manipulation, or coercion, or at the very least the reduction of the gospel to a commodity in a sales campaign. The gospel deserves better than that. A speaker at a World Council of Churches consultation a few years ago remarked that:

> Too often the Church has confused proclamation with words alone, forgetting the integral witness of worship, deed and life. Too often the Church has confounded witness with the imposition of a gospel wrapped in cultural trappings that obscure the living Christ.[2]

In this decade of the nineties we are reminded of a number of anniversaries, some of which have to do with the beginnings of European explorations of a wider world 500 years ago. We have been reminded of the voyages of Christopher Columbus. Early in the decade which saw Vasco da Gama sail around the Cape of Good Hope and open a sea route to the east for Europeans, Columbus took the wrong direction and found himself in the 'West Indies'. He did not, of course, *discover* the West Indies and South America: there were lots of people who knew very well that was where they lived, and they didn't need an Italian from Spain to tell them. But that piece of history is a sad reminder of ways in which a gospel wrapped in cultural trappings can obscure the living Christ. With the plunder of South America came the introduction of a slavery more vicious than anything the ancient world had known; the beginnings of a modern European racism which conveniently saw black and brown people as less than human, and so able to be exploited and mistreated with impunity. That was the worst kind of proselytism – a species of evangelism distorted beyond measure by an overwhelming concern with riches, and numbers and territory.

Compare that with the example of Jesus. In Matthew 8 there is a fascinating account of a meeting between a centurion and Jesus. The centurion had a servant at home who was 'racked with pain'. Jesus said he would go and see the man. That's not necessary, said the centurion. I have people under my command, and regularly say 'come here; do that', and they do. You too need only say the word, and my servant will be healed. The point of the passage emerges in the response of Jesus to that: 'Jesus heard him with astonishment, and said to the people who were following him, "Truly I tell you: nowhere in Israel have I found such faith. Many, I tell you, will come from east and west to sit with Abraham, Isaac, and Jacob at the banquet in the kingdom of Heaven."'

Faith is not confined to Israel, to the people of our religion, Jesus was saying. Others, from all corners of the world, have genuine religious faith, and so they will, as it were, join with Jewish people in the kingdom of heaven.

What does that mean for the preaching of the gospel? If it is not a sales campaign, or a process of conquest, what is it? Listen for a moment to William Johnston, a Jesuit who has worked in Japan for more than forty years as a teacher at Sophia University and a Christian with a profound concern for Christian–Buddhist dialogue. In a remarkable series of letters to friends, William Johnston wrote with great sensitivity and insight about issues in inter-religious dialogue. One of the letters is to an American university lecturer planning a visit to

Japan, who worried about the decline of missionary zeal in the church. Johnston wrote:

> Woe to me if I do not preach the Gospel! In dialogue we preach the entire Gospel because we love the Gospel, and want to share its treasures with people we love. We put no pressure on anyone to accept it. No beguiling promises. No stern threats. No charming enticements. No malicious bribes. No backstairs politics . . . And so it is entirely up to those who hear our word. They accept what they want; they leave what they don't want. We never break into the inner sanctum of conscience where the human person is alone with God. And this demands detachment . . . this is disinterested love.[3]

Isn't that a delightful thing to have written? Like Malachi, Johnston has found that in the farthest east God's name is great among the nations. He understands how dialogue and evangelism can go together; that meetings between people of different faiths can be mutually enriching. Jesus was astonished by the faith of a centurion, by the quality of religious perception and life found outside the boundaries drawn around his people. 'Nowhere in Israel have I found such faith,' he said. On that occasion, it was out in the wider world that faith was found.

How then are we to present the gospel, if we are also to be consistent with those examples? If we do not concentrate first and foremost on numbers, and income, and geographical expansion, what are we to concentrate on? When I first went to lecture in Brighton, in 1975, there was a gentle and scholarly man there called Kenneth Cragg. Author of many books on Muslim-Christian relationships, Kenneth Cragg had been an Anglican bishop in the Middle East and was then Reader in Religious Studies at the University of Sussex. In a book called *The Christian and Other Religion*, he argued that evangelism should not be concerned primarily with numbers or with geographical expansion, but with 'the increase of the Christlike person'. It's a lovely phrase. And it leaves open the possibility that Christ may speak *to* us as well as *through* us in our meetings with people of other faiths. When I read that, I remembered India, and Hindus I had met there. People who were knowledgeable about religion, sensitive to the faiths of others, deeply spiritual, and with great moral probity. They greatly enhanced my understanding of what religious faith can be, and so they also enhanced my understanding of Christian faith. I thought of Gandhi, and the problems he presented for a theology of mission as a man who lived the Sermon on the Mount much more directly than most Christians.

In meetings with people of other faiths, the aim is 'the increase of the Christlike person'. In *me* as well as in *them*. Whether the conversation is between Christian and Muslim, Christian and Jew, Christian and Hindu, Christian and Buddhist, the possibility is that there will be an increase of the Christlike person, on both sides.

Did you notice in the passage from Matthew 8 the sensitivity of the centurion? He was a member of a hated army of occupation. He was sufficiently open-minded to ask Jesus for help. But he was also sensitive enough to recognize the danger to the reputation of Jesus were he to visit his house. He put it very nicely when he said, 'Sir, I am not worthy to have you under my roof.' There was a sensitivity in him that should be present whenever people of different faiths meet. The main point of the passage has to do not with healing, but with the recognition of faith outside Israel. It also suggests that those of other faiths may be sensitive and perceptive; and that Jesus himself was not afraid to defy religious and social taboos in meeting those of other faiths. But there is also a warning here.

Following the suggestion that 'many will come from east and west to sit with Abraham, Isaac and Jacob' . . . there is the threat that 'those who were born to the kingdom will be thrown out into the dark' . . . In the context the warning was to those who claimed to be in the succession to Abraham: those who thought, 'we are all right; we are the ones who are in the know; we are the ones who will be saved, simply because we are descendants of Abraham'. And the rebuke of Jesus to them contrasts them with the centurion, and says: 'nowhere in Israel have I found such faith'. In reading that part of the passage we need to have about us a proper sensitivity to Judaism. The words of Jesus about Abraham's successors are not to be read as a condemnation of Jews, either in New Testament times or more especially now. Christians and Muslims are also descendants of Abraham. And if the words are taken to refer only or especially to Jews, they would have nothing to say to the rest of us. Like other texts of this kind, this can only have meaning for us if we apply the words to our own situations.

When we, as Christians, read that passage, we have to put ourselves into the picture it creates. We must ask: Do we, comparing ourselves with people of other faiths, say: 'I'm all right. I'm in the succession of Jesus. I'm a member of the church. I'm saved. But them . . . !' If we are tempted to do that, will we hear the words of Jesus addressed to people of other faith communities and saying: 'Nowhere among all my followers have I found such faith'?

Vincent Donovan, an American catholic, asked pertinently: 'What of those who cast aside their arrogance toward other human beings and cultures and religions and are gentle enough to be open to conversion? Are they not the ones "who shall inherit the earth"?'[4]

Whether in evangelism or dialogue, the aim does not have to do primarily with numbers, comforting as it may be to be wrapped around by a large congregation, and certainly the aim should not be geographical expansion – the 'planting' of yet more expensive property. The aim, both of evangelism and dialogue, is 'the increase of the Christlike person'.

14 The Rainbow

Rainbows, bright against the dark grey clouds, are always a remarkable sight. Just for a few moments we are allowed a glimpse into that whole spectrum of colours that is always there, but is normally invisible to human eyes. When we see the rainbow, we do what religious people and poets have always longed to do. We see the invisible. In the glow of colours we are able briefly to look beyond 'the little lights for which our bodily vision is made'.[1]

The rainbow – like many natural forces – was once taken to be a sign of God's activity. In Genesis 9 it is related to the idea of the covenant, which is a central biblical idea: 'Whenever the bow appears in the cloud, I shall see it and remember the everlasting covenant between God and living creatures of every kind on earth' (Gen. 9.16). God makes an agreement, a bargain, between himself and various groups of people. If they promise to trust and serve him, he will reward them or make use of them. So there is a covenant with the people of Israel. And Christians believe that there is a new covenant, spelled out in the New Testament, in which the church becomes a people bound to God, knowing that he is bound to them. We are used to thinking of two covenants: an Old Testament and a New Testament; a covenant with Israel and a covenant with the church. But there are more.

There is the covenant of Noah, a covenant with all humankind. There are covenants with Abraham and Moses, representatives of a particular people. There is the new covenant of Jeremiah, suggesting a more immediately personal relationship between the individual and God – 'I shall set my law within them, writing it on their hearts' (Jer. 31.33). And there

is the new covenant made through Jesus, sometimes understood
in terms like those expressed in John's Gospel: 'I am the true
vine, and my Father is the gardener . . . Anyone who dwells in
me, as I dwell in him, bears much fruit' (John 15.1, 5).

It is the first of those which appears in the passage from
Genesis 9, a covenant with all humankind made through Noah.
The story within which it is set is of course a mythical story,
bound up with the legend of a great flood. It is also the story
of Noah, who is said to have lived for 950 years; Noah, the first
successful agriculturalist, who planted a vineyard which did so
well that he got drunk on the proceeds. That led to a curse on
Canaan, who not accidentally represents the people whose
lands the Jews had occupied.

Many of these wonderful stories of Genesis were believed to
explain some of the circumstances of people's lives. In this story
of the rainbow, there is the belief that God has established his
covenant with *all* people. Like a shaft of light shining through
the clouds to produce the rainbow, here is a brief glimpse of a
belief, not consistently acknowledged, that God is indeed the
God of *all* people, everywhere and for all time. God has
declared that his love and his care extend to all humankind; and
the colours of the rainbow serve as a reminder of the variety of
people and cultures and nations encompassed by that love.

God is not to be seen as the God of one particular people,
but of all people. God is not the God of the British, or the
German, or the European only, but of all people. God is not
the God of the Protestant, or heaven forbid of Methodists
only, but of the Roman Catholics and the Eastern Orthodox
and the Anglicans. And God – here is what to some would seem
an audacious thought – is not God of Christians only, but of
people of all religions and none. For many Christians that is a
very difficult thought. Most of us are brought up, or brought
into the church, in the belief that there is an easy, inevitable
superiority about being a Christian, with the sometimes un-
spoken corollary that those who are not Christians are
somehow inferior. Most of us imbibe that belief, if not with our
mother's milk, then through our formative years of Christian

contact. And then we meet somebody of another faith. We get to know a Jew, or a Hindu, or a Muslim, and our too easy assumptions begin to crumble. We realize that our perceptions have been too limited. Just as, having seen sun and rain, we are surprised to see a rainbow with the colours that had been there all the time but not visible to us, so we are surprised at the discovery that deep spirituality, high moral probity and real religious understanding are to be found among people of many different faiths. The qualities had been there all the time, but we had not been able to see them.

Is there something in our traditions which makes it difficult for us to see that particular rainbow? Consider for a moment a New Testament reference to a controversy between Jesus and some Pharisees. Jesus was invited to a meal in a Pharisee's house, but offended his host by sitting down to eat without first washing. The text has him saying:

> You Pharisees clean the outside of cup and plate; but inside you are full of greed and wickedness. You fools! Did not he who made the outside make the inside too? . . . Alas for you Pharisees! You pay tithes of mint and rue and every kind of garden herb, but neglect justice and the love of God. It is these you should have practised without neglecting the others (Luke 11.39–42).

It is the kind of passage that has been used to support the view that Jews and Judaism are legalistic about religion, concerned with minute details and scrupulous observance of laws and traditions, unlike Christians, who have the grace and the love of God to save them from such things. That kind of comparison is a parody, although it has been commonplace among too many Christians for far too long. Jews know about the love of God. After all, it was the Jewish law which Jesus quoted when he said that the greatest of all commandments is to love God and love your neighbour. And Jesus was close to the Pharisees, perhaps closer to them than to other Jewish groups of the time. He agreed with them in matters of theology.[2] He agreed with them that the poor and pious of Israel, rather than the rich and powerful collaborators with Rome, were the true inheritors of the promises of God. He agreed with them that the law should be carefully observed: 'so long as earth and heaven endure, not a letter, not a dot, will disappear from the law . . .' (Matt. 5.18). There is little doubt that he and the Pharisees agreed on the things which were of the greatest importance – love, mercy, justice, charity – those things which the Hebrew Bible emphasized as of primary importance.

So why were the Pharisees given such a bad press? I think you can only make sense of the Gospel material if you accept that what we have in the Gospels is an intertwining of at least two things: recollections of what Jesus said and did, and what the church was making of that in their own situations thirty, forty, fifty, maybe eighty years after the events. There is a fusion in New Testament material between the stories of Jesus handed down as Christians met to worship, and the teaching which was developed out of those stories and related to the daily lives and circumstances of the early Christians.

One of the burning issues of the earliest church had to do with whether or to what extent Christians should observe Jewish rules and follow Jewish practices. Paul's Letters and the Acts of the Apostles contain many references to that controversy. In discussing and arguing with one another, Christians appear to have projected back into the time of Jesus the later arguments about whether people who appeared to take Jewish law too seriously were being self-righteous, and were concerned too much with empty formalities. The scribes and the Pharisees became the foil for Christian ideas in those arguments as early Christian interpreters in effect said: 'we have love, mercy, repentance, forgiveness and even simple decency on our side, and that is why our religion is superior to its parent'.[3]

Can the rainbow shed light on what is written about Jesus and the Pharisees? We have the story of Noah, and the early covenant, claiming that God is indeed the God of *all* people; of *all* cultures; of *all* religions. And that bright bow shining against the clouds can still remind us that we can share with and learn from people of other traditions and faiths. My personal experience in India long ago taught me that Christian faith can be enriched by encounters with people of other faiths. But many Christians seem to be frightened by the thought of close encounters with people of other faiths. Perhaps they find it simpler and more comforting to ignore the challenges. And it may be tempting to fall back on some features of Christian tradition which appear dismissive of non-Christian religions. The passage from Luke 11 raises a concern about ways in which stories about Jesus and the Pharisees were written up and used in later Christian life. There is an insidious seed there which if allowed to grow will produce the thought: 'I can only value my own religious faith if in doing so I denigrate the faith of other people.'

In Luke Jesus is seen arguing with *his own* traditions, with other Jews. Is it difficult for us now to acknowledge that the founder of Christianity knew nothing of 'Christians', or 'Christianity', or the churches? That he lived and died purely within a Jewish milieu? He was arguing with his own traditions, and within them was especially concerned to emphasize pictures of a God who saves sinners, a God of love and mercy, of forgiveness and acceptance. The early church accepted his message, and on the whole lived by it. But some seem to have been unable to shake off the tendency to target someone else, to find someone else to denigrate and deny, as if expressing a need to say: 'only if they are wrong can I be right.'

There may be a psychological explanation for this. It is a fact of psychology, as I understand it, that we tend to condemn most strongly in others the things we should most like to do ourselves. We probably do not condemn the mass murderer with any real sense of moral outrage. We are puzzled by his actions, but we are not tempted to do such things ourselves. They seem simply inexplicable. But somebody doing what, even if not conscious of it we would love to do ourselves were we not too inhibited – ah, that is likely to infuriate us. We are jealous, not of people who do the things we could never do, but of those who succeed where we so nearly could. We tend to condemn in others – all unconsciously, of course – the things we would really like to do ourselves. Starting from Noah, and then puzzling over how to read the stories of controversies between Jesus and the Pharisees, we ask 'is there a religious version of this?' Is there a tendency to say, 'my confidence in my own correctness, my own virtue, is in part dependent upon denigrating others?'

Jesus, we must remember, was very close to the Pharisees of his day. And as a good Jew he seemed to have delighted in arguing and debating with his fellow Jews. The teaching of Jesus, as we receive it, is constantly questioning, teasing out, asking: 'does this practice or that interpretation really reflect the justice and the love of God?' The probing and the questioning and the debating of Jesus was carried on within his own Jewish tradition, but was also pointing forward. Forward to an emphasis upon essentials rather than upon trivia; forward to a faith which focussed upon the justice and the love of God. But it had its roots in a distant past. And it connected with the story of a rainbow, as a reminder of the love of God for all people, everywhere, at all times. There is hope in the rainbow. Do you remember how D. H. Lawrence expressed that in the conclusion to his novel of that name? His heroine Ursula had experienced and suffered so much. Yet at the end of it all, she saw hope of something new, a new creation:

> She saw in the rainbow the earth's new architecture, the old, brittle corruption of houses and factories swept away, the world built up in a living fabric of Truth, fitting to the over-arching heaven.[4]

As we think of the rainbow, perhaps we too can imagine how the brittle corruption which uses religion to divide and destroy can be transformed into a harmony beneath the over-arching heaven, where God's love extends to all his creatures.

> Whenever the bow appears in the cloud, I shall see it and remember the everlasting covenant between God and living creatures of every kind on earth.

15 The Landowner and the Vineyard

In Luke's Gospel there is a parable about a man who 'planted a vineyard, let it out to vinegrowers, and went abroad for a long time' (20.9).

Silly man, we might say. If he cared about his land and his vines, why didn't he stay to look after them? Of course, one shouldn't take parables too literally. But this one does seem to require more than the usual amount of unpacking. The first thought that ran through my mind as I considered this passage was, 'who owns the land?' That was quickly followed by: 'under what conditions should people expect to own land?'

British people, in common with most Europeans, have had strange views about land which have often collided with quite different ideas found in other parts of the world. Take, for example, the view that large areas of land can be privately owned, and others refused access to them or allowed access only if they pay. That is by no means a universal idea. When the British first arrived in North America they encountered Indians who had quite different ways of thinking about land. For them, land was common. As semi-nomadic peoples, they could roam across it. They might occasionally come into conflict with another tribe or group who wanted to keep them out of a particular area, but that would not be on the grounds that individuals could own the land. The thought of owning land, on the European model, was as foreign to them as the idea of somebody claiming to own the air. But the British had become accustomed to the view that large areas of land could be owned by private individuals. It could be closed off and fenced in; people who lived on the land could be thrown off it and its natural resources could be denied to the population at large.

Land, and the ownership of land, represent both wealth and power. You and I can no longer go freely and stand at Land's End, gazing out at the Atlantic. Somebody owns Lands End, and if we want to step on to that part of our national heritage, we have to pay to do so.

To some people, that seemed a very strange idea. After the Battle of Plassey, in 1757, the British for the first time came into control of a large tract of Indian territory. They began to administer land in Bengal. Their predecessors, the great Moghul Emperors, had done the same. The Moghuls had often been very tough in the way they collected the taxes levied on land and crops. People who failed to pay their dues were sometimes treated very harshly. What would never have happened is that they would have been thrown off the land they tended as a punishment for non-payment. The British, accustomed to the ways these things were done in Europe, introduced the idea that individuals could own the land, and that therefore defaulters could be ejected from it. If they could not pay their taxes at the time they would never have the chance to pay them in future, because they would no longer have the opportunity of producing. It was a novel idea.[1]

I mention that simply to start a strain or two of thought running around this parable of the vineyard. It tells of an absentee landlord, who from his Swiss tax haven, or wherever he lived, sent an agent once a year to collect his dues. We can imagine the people who did all the work on the land getting a bit fed up with that. What's more, under Jewish law it would seem that there was a presumption of ownership on the part of those who had possession of the property.[2] So did the tenants have a point? They shouldn't have killed people, but their motives in wanting to protect the land they worked might have been splendidly pure.

That's all very well, but this is a parable, is it not? It is, but it is not made up of the ordinary everyday events and incidents which are found in most of the parables. It appears to be more allegory than parable. So why is the story told in this way, and recorded as a significant part of the teaching of Jesus?

Essentially, the story is about the rejection and death of the prophets, whose message often went unheeded. In the time of Jesus, that would have been the likeliest and most pertinent understanding of it. Chafing with frustration at the religious leaders of the day, and urgently wanting his own message to be heard by the people, Jesus drew a parallel with the prophets, and put it into this rather strange story about property rights, and absentee landlords, and rebellious tenants. It had happened that prophets had been rejected in the past. Jesus put that experience in colourful and trenchant terms. 'So they flung him out of the vineyard and killed him.' The same kind of thing, he seems to suggest, could happen to him.

Then there is added a quotation about the stone which the builders rejected: probably an addition by the early church, with the implication, drawn out in Matthew's version, that 'the kingdom of God will be taken away from you and given to a nation that yields the proper fruit'. That addition is for me the problem with the whole passage, even as it is found in Mark and Luke. It contains an incipient anti-Jewishness. A common but too simple Christian interpretation is that the kingdom of God – justice and righteousness, religious truth and a true morality – will be taken from the Jewish people and given instead to 'a nation that yields the proper fruit', that is, to the Christian church. In their failure to convert the Jews and their struggle against the Pharisees' interpretation of scripture, the early church wrote into that passage the belief that Christianity must supersede Judaism. The consequences, however, are far greater than Christians of that time could have anticipated, and we now have to look again and more carefully at texts of this kind. It should be impossible for a sensitive, informed Christian, looking back on centuries of antisemitism, not to feel a shudder of revulsion at texts which have lent themselves to an anti-Jewish interpretation. At its heart, ours is a gospel of love and grace and acceptance. It cannot stand on a programme of rejection and vilification, regarding itself as a faith which exists because another faith is destroyed.

How, then, are we to read the parable? The story as Jesus

probably told it was a protest against religious leaders. What needed to grow in the vineyards he was concerned with was not religious authorities, or tradition, or hierarchies, but the harvest of his teaching. If there is a message for us in this passage, it has to do with that same theme, rather than with a kind of anti-Jewishness. For Jesus, the protest is against an authoritarian kind of religion which imposes burdens, creates guilt, but offers no liberation. It is a protest that led to his own rejection and crucifixion. How strange, then, that Christians have sometimes made of Jesus the very kind of rigid authoritarian figure he condemned.

The great French writer Albert Camus wrote a novel called *The Plague [La Peste]*, about an outbreak of Bubonic plague in a north African town, and people's reactions to the terrors it caused. In the story it is actually the less religious people who come out best. They do so by displaying the kinds of qualities we see in Jesus himself. The hero of the book, Dr Rieux, vigorously directs medical operations even though he recognizes that the cause is hopeless. There is a character called Tarrou, who says he would like to be 'a saint without God'. He organizes squads to patrol the streets and find victims of the plague. Rambert, a journalist who at first plans to escape from the plague-stricken town in order to save himself, then decides that 'it may be shameful to be happy by oneself'.

It is sacrificial service which characterizes those men. The priest comes out of it less well. His initial response is to say that the plague must be God's will and so people must submit to it. 'Plague,' he says, 'is the flail of God in the world, his threshing floor.' People should accept it as a divine judgment. The priest dies with his face turned to the wall. The others decide to lose themselves in works of compassion. They conclude that 'The honour of man begins with his willingness to offer himself in sacrificial death'.[3]

In Luke 9 there is a reference to Jesus starting his journey to Jerusalem: ' . . . he set his face resolutely towards Jerusalem, and sent messengers ahead. They set out and went into a Samaritan village to make arrangements for him; but the villagers would not receive him, because he was on his way to Jerusalem' (Luke 9.51–53).

The passion of Jesus had already begun when he set his face towards Jerusalem. Perhaps we think of that in terms of Jesus being sent to a heroic conflict and eventual triumph by the will of God, with his evil opponents equally bound by the divine purpose. But consider the possibility of Jesus as a rebel, in some ways like the characters in *The Plague*. He was after all a critic of false absolutes: of rules and rituals and hierarchical control. In place of those things, the absolute which Jesus embodied and actualized was love, shown in his works of heal-ing and feeding, in his refusal to coerce, in expecting those who followed him to make their own choices and take up the cross on their own account. In the end, Jesus had to be willing to die if he did not want to compromise with that absolute.

The love Jesus embodies was characterized not by the exercise of arbitrary power, nor by the imposition of rules and formulas, but by their opposites: by self-giving and in iden-tification with those whom respectable society excluded. In the story by Camus there is a scene in which an old man is looking in a shop window at Christmas time, and remembering his wife years ago, before she left him. Dr Rieux, looking at him,

> knew also, what the old man was thinking, as his tears flowed, and he, Rieux, thought it too: that a loveless world is a dead world, and always there comes an hour when one is weary of . . . one's work, and of devotion to duty, and all one craves for is a loved face, the warmth and wonder of a loving heart.[4]

As the embodiment of the divine love, Jesus set his face resolutely towards Jerusalem, towards suffering and death. In a world in which both religious and political absolutes – false absolutes – were imposed harshly and unimaginatively, the only way he could hold on to that one true absolute of love was by his suffering and death. 'The villagers would not receive him because he had set his face towards Jerusalem.' Prophets may be rejected, perhaps even killed. Such was the case with Jesus. Do we too refuse to receive him, because he set his face towards Jerusalem?

Peace

16 Racial Justice in an Unequal World

The last fifty years have witnessed a dramatic change to the place of the British people in the world. It is a change we do not often discuss openly, and as a result it induces xenophobia and hostility to newcomers in too many of us. Of course the situation of people in this country has changed dramatically in many ways over the last fifty years. But the change we rarely talk about is bound up with our loss of empire. How strange it is to reflect that in the 1920s and 1930s a quarter of the world's land surface and a quarter of the world's population were incorporated into the British Empire. Our maps were generously splashed with the red of Britain's possessions; our sons (or rather, the sons of an élite) could go from their public schools or Oxbridge to far-flung corners of the world to take up positions of responsibility and power; British commerce had captive markets and assured sources of raw materials. It was indeed a different world.

Now it has gone. The only remnants are the Falkland Islands and for a few months more Hong Kong. Kipling wrote long before the event, but with unerring prophecy:

> The tumult and the shouting dies;
>   The Captains and the Kings depart . . .
>
> Far-called, our navies melt away;
>   On dune and headland sinks the fire:
> Lo, all our pomp of yesterday
>   Is one with Ninevah and Tyre![1]

The Empire has gone; but the Empire has also come to live

among us. Why do people find that so hard to deal with? The
issues, after all, are not simply to do with immigration. At the
height of the debates on immigration policy, in the 1960s and
1970s, the majority of immigrants arriving in Britain were
white, from the 'Old Commonwealth', Europe and America.[2] It
was also a time when more people left the United Kingdom than
entered it. Yet the public debate about immigration has been
couched almost entirely in terms of the threat posed to Britain
by a 'tide' of black and coloured immigrants which if unchecked
would overwhelm the country. The fact that most immigrants
since the Second World War have been white has passed un-
noticed. The word 'immigrant' itself has come to be used as a
synonym for 'black' or coloured'. The young black teenager
whose grandparents were immigrants and whose parents were
born in Britain will still be regarded by many as an 'immigrant'.
Yet white politicians whose parents were immigrants can be
regarded as part of the establishment, as can members of the
Royal Family who are first-generation immigrants. Why should
that be so?

I suspect that such attitudes are bound up with a now half-
forgotten or falsely remembered past. A past in which even
those who never stepped beyond the shores of Britain
could regard themselves as superior because they belonged to a
successful, imperial, nation. It was the British who went to
distant lands to rule over and subordinate the natives. The dark
places of the world could only be enlightened by the white man
or woman. Those attitudes entered deeply into the unconscious
mind of the British people. So there were problems with people
who came, or whose parents came, from the ex-Empire. It was
one thing for the sons of middle and upper-class Britain to
travel the Empire road; it was quite another to have travellers
come in the opposite direction and move in next door. The
white British have a problem with racial attitudes.

Where are we to look for a Christian view of race relations?
In the Old Testament, we find an ambivalent set of ideas. In
places there runs strongly the theme of a vital, even violent,
Jewish nationalism; in other places what is commended is

tolerance and acceptance of alien people. But it might be no bad thing to begin with the decalogue, the ten commandments, and to notice that the ninth commandment decrees that 'You shall not bear false witness against your neighbour' (Deut. 5.20). Is that something to beware of in our dealings with people of other races, religions and cultures? Are we tempted sometimes to indulge in the crude stereotyping which gives false evidence of our neighbours' beliefs or moral attitudes? The ninth commandment for us today might well include a requirement to understand sympathetically the beliefs and values of Jew and Muslim and Sikh and Hindu, and to recognize the great variety of people who are encompassed by overarching words like 'black', 'Asian', 'West Indian'.

A good set of readings to help a reflection on race relations can then be found in the Book of Ruth. It's a wonderful story, and a great piece of protest writing. It is widely thought to have been written at the same time as the books of Ezra and Nehemiah, that is when the Jewish nation was being re-established with the return of those who had been exiled in Babylonia. Many Jewish authorities were trying to push the people back into a sense of a 'pure' Jewishness, discouraging mixed marriages. It was against that background that the story of Ruth was written.

The book begins with economic migrants, as Elimelech, Naomi and their two sons move from Bethlehem in famine-stricken Judah to Moabite country. Evidently the Moabites did not have restrictive immigration and asylum laws, and so the family settled down. The two sons married Moabite women – Orpah and Ruth. After ten years the sons died, and Naomi decided she should return to her old home in Bethlehem. She advised her widowed daughters to stay in their own country, where they would surely have a better chance of finding new husbands among their own ethnic group than in the land of Judah. Orpah kissed her mother-in-law and took her leave. Ruth had other ideas, expressed in the memorable words: 'Do not urge me to go back and desert you. Where you go, I shall go, and where you stay I shall stay. Your people will be my people, and your God my God. Where you die I shall die, and there be buried. I solemnly declare before the Lord that nothing but death will part me from you' (Ruth 1.16f.).

Ruth herself then became a migrant. Like many first-generation immigrants, she had to take what work she could get. The barley harvest was just beginning, and there was an opportunity for seasonal work. Ruth asked her mother-in-law: 'May I go to the harvest fields and glean behind anyone who will allow me?' So she joined in the work of harvesting, and there in the fields she met Boaz. Her mother-in-law was not slow to give her advice about how Ruth could make herself attractive to Boaz: 'Bathe and anoint yourself with perfumed oil, then get dressed and go down to the threshing floor; but do not make yourself known to the man until he has finished eating and drinking.'

It is a romantic story, and it comes swiftly to its natural conclusion. Ruth and Boaz became husband and wife, and soon a son was born to them. That brings us to the punch line, and to the conclusion of the story. Her son, Obed, was the father of Jesse, who in turn was the father of David, the greatest king of Israel. Do you see what the story is saying? At a time when xenophobia was rife, and Jews were encouraged to think of inter-marriage with people of other nations as a kind of apostasy, the beautiful story of Ruth points out that the great-grandmother of one of Israel's greatest sons was not a Jew, but a Moabitess – Ruth the *goy*.

The book was a wonderful protest, but a Christian theology of race relations requires more than a lovely Old Testament story to give it credibility. And there are pointers in the New Testament to things which undergird good relationships between people of different races and cultures and creeds. The great fallacy of racial prejudice is to regard *all* members of another group as the same. Yet a notable characteristic of Jesus was that he treated each person as an individual, unique in the sight of God and precious on that account. In his vivid and picturesque way he expressed the thought by saying: 'even the hairs of your head have all been counted' (Luke 12.7).

Paul took up a similar theme when he declared: 'There is no such thing as Jew and Greek, slave and freeman, male and female; for you are all one person in Jesus Christ' (Gal. 3.28).[3] We might add, 'there is no such thing from a Christian perspective as Anglo-Saxon or West Indian, Celt or Norman or Asian, because we all share a common humanity'. Might it be that our nation's colonial past makes it especially difficult for us to recognize the implications of such teaching? Racist attitudes formed in imperial situations are very hard to eradicate. The Empire has gone; but the Empire has come to live among us. And that is a bitter pill to swallow for many British people who have only the slightest notion of our imperial history.

Happily, there is another spin-off of colonial expansion which has been quite different. That is something which was discovered in the mission of the church, at its best. In preaching the gospel around the world, building hospitals and schools, helping people to a better life, the church has discovered that to give is also to receive. It has found in its own experience that gift of fellowship, of *koinonia*, in which men and women whose nationality, race, and background are very different become one in the service of the gospel.

In Luke's Gospel there is that familiar story of the Good Samaritan (10.30–37). It was told in answer to a question which was intended to dig a little deeper into the commandment to 'love your neighbour as yourself'. 'But who is my neighbour?' was the entirely proper question asked by an expert in the law. It was characteristic of Jesus – have you noticed? – that he did not reply with a direct answer. There was no attempt at a definition. Instead, Jesus told a story. The story of a man travelling from Jerusalem to Jericho who was set upon by robbers, who took everything he had and left him wounded by the roadside. Traditionally respected religious figures left the man where he was, and hurried by on the other side of the road. Then came the Samaritan, who bandaged his wounds, took him to an inn, and paid for his care until he had recovered. The story ended with a question. Who was it who acted as a neighbour to the man who fell among robbers? That required the audience to consider an answer so prepostorous that it might well have shocked them into recognition of a new idea. The hero of the story Jesus told was a despised schismatic, a Samaritan, a person most unlikely to have been commended by a Jew. That was the sting in the story. Being a neighbour was not dependent upon any natural relationship. It was dependent upon being in a position to understand and befriend and help, without regard to religious barriers or bigotry.

Within the fellowship of the church it is possible to demonstrate the unity of people of different races. The church is intended to be a sign of the new humanity, a model of a community where at last God is seen to dwell among all humanity, and is recognized in the faces of people of all races and creeds and ethnic groups.

17 War and Peace

According to John's Gospel, when Jesus greeted the disciples after the resurrection he used the traditional Jewish greeting (20.19). It is rendered in English as 'Peace be with you!', a direct translation of the Greek words *Eirene humin*. But the word *eirene* for peace is itself simply a translation of the common Hebrew greeting, *shalom*.[1] Go to a meeting of your local Council of Christians and Jews (as I hope you will sometime), and you will hear people greeting each other with the word *shalom*.

As a conventional greeting shalom means something like 'may all be well with you'. But the word also suggests peace, harmony, prosperity; a state of total well-being, untroubled by violence. Shalom includes the idea of a long life of happiness, free from destructive violence and ending in a natural death. Part of the promise to Abraham was: 'You yourself will join your forefathers in peace and be buried at a ripe old age' (Gen. 15.15). Shalom is also part of the dream of a messianic kingdom, when 'nation will not lift sword against nation nor ever again be trained for war' (Isa. 2.4). Shalom is established in communities, and is regarded as a gift of family life which may be extended to nations.

When Jesus said to his disciples, 'Peace be with you' they would have recognized not the Christianizing of a concept into a Greek word but the resonances of the Hebrew *shalom*. Although John wrote, 'the disciples were together behind locked doors *for fear of the Jews*', let's not forget that Jesus and his disciples were themselves Jews, with no thoughts at the time of any alternative religion. Shalom, peace, was a gift offered to the disciples, and a gift the disciples were to carry out into the world.The disciples already knew that those who make peace are in a special sense to be called the children of God. 'Blessed are the peacemakers; they shall be called God's children' (Matt. 5.9). The peacemakers are called God's children because they reproduce something of the character of God in their own lives. But the peace of the Sermon on the Mount is a costly peace, built of sacrifice and suffering and forgiving love. In the symbolism of John's story, that gives added significance to the way in which the greeting from Jesus is followed by him showing his disciples his hands and his side. The marks of the crucifixion testify that it is Jesus who is risen, but they also point to the cost of the true shalom.

What might shalom mean for us, in relation to the great issues of war and peace? We need to think about such a question calmly, and well in advance of any actual conflict. By the time a war breaks out or a conflict arises the fog of propaganda will already have obscured the moral issues. I am reminded of an American historian of South Asia who, describing the surprisingly sudden defeat of the British at Singapore in the Second World War, when the defenders waited behind huge guns pointing out to sea as the advancing army came overland behind them, wrote that the 'Japanese army . . . caught Britain's command with their gin and tonics half-down'.[2] For us the problem may not be gin and tonics; but might we be caught with our ideas about war and peace only half-digested?

There is a long tradition of Christian thinking about war and peace which in origin goes back to the Greeks but in its Christian form has influenced international conventions and moral thinking for centuries. That is the Just War doctrine, a set of principles designed to provide moral guidance on reasons which might justify the use of war in certain circumstances, and which also suggest rules that should apply if war occurs. The title 'Just War' is much derided by people who assume that the doctrine mindlessly approves of war and regards it as a good thing. Not so. The intentions of the Just War teaching are to prevent wars from occurring whenever possible, and to limit their horrors when they do. Many of these principles have been incorporated into international law and agreements, and where that has happened they are no longer simply theological ideas.

So what is this Christan teaching about war and peace? It begins by acknowledging that there might be circumstances in which it would be right to defend territory or people against an aggressor. But it has much more to say than that. It says, reasonably enough, that there should be no declaration of war until every attempt to prevent it has failed. War should always be a last resort. It suggests that there should be a proportionality between the evil that would be caused by fighting a war and the good that would be achieved in eventual victory. Before embarking upon war, people should consider what their aims are, and whether the achievement of such aims could outweigh all the evil that war will inevitably bring in its wake. The Just War rules also require that there should be 'moral certainty' that the cause of justice will emerge victorious. And as far as the conduct of war is concerned, it demands a proper respect for neutrals and no deliberate attacks on non-combatants.

We need to recognize some very important and perhaps puzzling things about this set of moral principles. They include a responsible weighing of the balance between the good to be achieved and the evil that will be caused; and 'moral certainty' that the cause of justice will emerge victorious. A balance that weighs more heavily in the direction of the good to be achieved than in the horrors to be endured. Is it a curious fact – although fact it certainly is – that the Just War teaching does not condone fighting wars for principles? If we listened only to the speeches of politicians as a nation prepared for war we could be excused for thinking that the only objective was to preserve a great principle – to defend democracy, to defeat communism, to fight a war to end all wars. That is how people are encouraged to fight. But how is one to know when such a cause has been achieved? Does it require wiping out the enemy, dispossessing him of everything, leaving him with no hope?

In retrospect, most wars are much less pure in intention, and the ironies if not the cynicism of political flag-waving become apparent. Did we really join with Saudi Arabia in order to defend democracy, or self-determination, in Kuwait? In the case of the Falklands the irony was that political speeches had made much of the need to defend the rights of British citizens in far-flung corners of the world. Only later was it realized that the British Nationality Act of 1982 had removed rights of entry to Britain from many 'non-patrial' Falkland Islanders, and special legislation was introduced in 1983 to restore the rights for which by then British troops had fought and died.[3]

People like to believe they are fighting for principles. But the Just War teaching does not encourage them to do that, precisely because diplomacy, common sense, and reason can only apply to wars fought for limited and recognizable ends. The historian Herbert Butterfield once remarked that wars for righteousness, as he called them, are almost always worse than wars fought for more limited ends.

> The implications of the 'war for righteousness' are that compromise becomes impossible, the original defensive object is superseded, the war becomes a war of unlimited ends . . . we have given war itself a greatly magnified role in history and in the processes of time.[4]

To declare, as politicians so often cannot resist declaring, that we have to go to war in order to defend abstract principles, is not a Christian attitude, whatever else it may be. In significant ways it contradicts Christian teaching. If you will pardon my quoting the inelegant language of a former President of the United States,[5] to go to war in order to *kick some ass* is not something sanctioned by Christian teaching, however tempting it may be in the face of frustrating and protracted political situations in which aggressive and murderous people appear to be getting away with their crimes.

Through the cacophony of sounds which will come to us through the media and from political leaders in times of crisis, we have to try to hear that shalom which is spoken to us in greeting by our Lord. And then we have an obligation to set out what Christian teaching actually says about peace. How it sets out principles of limited ends to any who would embark upon a war. How it declares the need to guard with great care the rights of neutrals and non-combatants, avoiding therefore deliberate attacks on civilian populations. How it puts into the heads of servicemen and women a clear idea of the morality of war, of rights and wrongs which still apply even in extreme circumstances and regardless of orders to the contrary. None of this is party political. It is simply a statement of the carefully constructed and long-standing Christian moral principles about war. If you find it uncomfortable or even offensive, please consider the possibility that the gospel is bound in certain respects to be challenging and troublesome.

One of the great figures of the twentieth century, in both religion and politics, is Mahatma Gandhi. Although not a Christian, Gandhi embodied to a remarkable degree many Christian virtues. For most of his life he was involved in conflict, in resistance to discrimination in South Africa and then as the greatest leader of the independence movement in India between 1920 and 1947. Gandhi worked out and practised a system of non-violent resistance and oppression based not only on his own Hindu background but also upon his reading of the Sermon on the Mount and of Christian writers. One of the principles he regarded as of primary importance in any conflict was the willingness to compromise. A protagonist in a conflict had to recognize from the beginning that in the end any solution would have to involve compromise. So he must allow his opponent room for manoeuvre and the opportunity to withdraw from positions without losing face. The art of compromise, in that sense, is an important ingredient in personal relationships, and is vital in international affairs.

Sadly, Gandhi's life ended when he was assassinated by Nathuram Vinayak Godse, a member of a right-wing Hindu group, the Hindu Mahasabha, who objected to Gandhi's compromises with Muslims and Christians, and wished to see Hinduism clearly established as the foremost religion of the new India.[6] Part of our struggle in times of conflict is bound to be with people of religious persuasion whose religion is bound up with simplistic slogans and the expectation that the 'war for righteousness' can succeed in doing good. In that struggle, we may lean not only on common sense and reason – early casualties of war as they are – but also on the words and teaching of Jesus. When we huddle behind locked doors, a minority of peacemakers in a belligerent world, perhaps we shall hear the echo of his greeting: *shalom* ; peace be with you.

18 A Peace Dividend?

Micah, an ancient prophet of Israel, recognized that peace and disarmament go together as surely as do armaments and war. In words that resound in our time as much as in his, he declared that God:

Shall judge between many peoples,
and shall decide for strong nations afar off;
and they shall beat their swords into ploughshares,
and their spears into pruning hooks;
nation shall not lift up sword against nation,
neither shall they learn war anymore (4.3).

Year after year around the world we see how military action in distant places is fuelled by arms supplied by Western arms traders. Europe might have experienced only very limited and brief military adventures between the Second World War and the outbreak of fighting in the former Yugoslavia, but it contributed mightily to other people's wars elsewhere. Most armaments for the more than three hundred wars fought since 1945 have been supplied by the USA and the USSR; the UK has the dubious distinction of being among the leaders of the rest of the world in exporting arms to the world's trouble spots.

As we now know, Britain was busily selling equipment for arms to Iraq until just before the Gulf War.[1] Americans were at one time funding semtex and guns for the IRA – we hope they are not still doing so, but how would we know? Leading politicians have regarded the sale of arms as an essential part of their strategy for improving Britain's balance of payments, and if the Press is to be believed at least one has not flinched from helping her own kith and kin to make a few million in the process. These are not arms produced to defend this country; nor to defend the weak and helpless of the world. These have been weapons produced simply in order to make a profit for somebody.

In Micah's time the prospect of beating swords into ploughshares and spears into pruning hooks was likely to have aroused less fears about the economic consequences than it would do today. It wasn't hopes of a peace dividend but the expectation of God's rule which prompted Micah to utter his prophecy about nations not having to learn war any more. They would be able to abandon weapons, he said, because it would be God who would judge many peoples; in God's reign of justice and righteousness there would be no further need for war. It was a vision. A lovely dream. Yet the visionary nature of Micah's words does not allow us to ignore them or set them aside. They are part of the great tradition of the Jewish prophets which has inspired and guided Christian ethical thinking from the beginning, as they inspired Jesus. Part of the art and the labour of following Jesus is the turning of dreams into reality; of taking the words of the prophets and of Jesus himself and making of them a manifesto of Christian action in our own time.

In some parts of the country there is a temptation not to be too critical of the unrestrained selling of arms because of that uneasy feeling that local industries will suffer if the trade declines. Of course we don't want even more people put out of work. But if that argument is used against us, let us remember that there are plenty of other, and more useful, things to produce; many other ways of giving people work. We have only to think of the industrial and commercial success of nations like Japan that have not peddled arms to see the hollowness of that particular defence against criticism.

To take one example, Bristol workers have a vested interest in the arms industry, and presumably that interest will increase as the monstrosity at Parkway comes into use. There, next to a major computer company and close to the University of the West of England, the huge buildings of the Defence Procurement Executive are rising. How much fuss would the churches have made, I wonder, if it had been something connected with the more common use of the word 'procurer' that was housed out there near Bristol Parkway station?

We know it is a delicate issue locally. Members of Parliament and people from constituencies where arms are produced – or is procured the right word? – tend to be less enthusiastic about disarmament. But being sensitive to their feelings and their fears does not mean ignoring the issues about disarmament which confront us in our newspapers and in the words of the prophets alike. We cannot allow so important a debate to be clouded by so immediate an interest. After all, in the eighteenth century Bristol's lucrative involvement in the slave trade was defended precisely on the grounds that it would be ruinous to get rid of it. Never mind the morality. Count the cost!

It is always difficult to give up things that are to our economic advantage. How much more so today, when our society, as it has developed, has made the profits of shareholders so much the criterion of economic and political action that it has become almost impossible to take into account the interests of other parties, let alone the dictates of morality. Never mind the prophets of Israel; just look to the profits of shareholders. Around the time that his book, *The State We're In*[2] was published, and well before it became a best-seller, Will Hutton gave the Benjamin Meaker Public lectures in the University of Bristol.[3] I managed to get to all three of them, and the effort was well rewarded. Part of Will Hutton's argument in that book is now well known because of the way in which the term 'stakeholder' has been taken up by the Labour Party. The lectures of this Bristol graduate gave a clear outline of his arguments well in advance of the publicity he was later to receive. A major part of his argument was that what he termed 'neo-classical capitalism' has been allowed so to dominate both society and the economy that nobody other than shareholders can now influence economic or political decisions – and even shareholders cannot do that very effectively. No other stakeholders can have a say. There is no say for passengers if the transport system is to be sold for a song in the market place; no say for patients (except through their wallets) if consultants have to be bribed to operate next week rather than next year; and certainly no say for the targets, the casualties, if arms are sold simply in order to make a profit.

There *are* other stakeholders. There are those involved in research and development, including all those who would prefer to be involved in more useful research. In industry in this country, 25% of all research and development is connected with military uses. In Government research, the figure is 45%. That compares with an overall 32% in France; 12% in Germany; and 5% in Japan.[4] But has there not been a peace dividend, in this as in other areas? Yes, there has. Between 1987 and 1993 military research and development was reduced by 4.4%. Aren't you glad about that? If you are, don't get ecstatic about it! Over the same period, civilian research and development was cut by 15%. And in spite of the peace dividend, 25% of Britain's electronics and information technology graduates are involved in the arms industry. What a terrible temptation with which to face new graduates. The prospect of a job in the arms industry, or perhaps no job at all. No wonder that half of Parkway needs to be laid waste to procure that lot, or that Japan and Germany have performed much better commercially and industrially than we have.

What about that now familiar word, stakeholders? What of the interests and needs of other parties beside the shareholders who have a stake in the arms industry? Could it be that arms production and trading today is not after all in our own commercial interests? That if we were to follow the example of Germany and Japan in devoting much more of our scientific expertise to civilian and commercial activity we should as a nation be better off? Certainly jobs are tied up with the arms industry at the moment. But Micah's dream of swords into ploughshares and spears into pruning hooks is not simply a relic of two-and-a-half thousand years ago. There are ways, as other countries demonstrate, to harness the inventiveness and productivity of industry to produce more useful, or at least less harmful, things.

The stakeholders are not only those involved in research, who perhaps would like their research to be in more productive areas if the money were available. They are not only the people who work in the arms industry, or those who make profits out of it. They are also the ones on whom the whole business impacts most seriously: people injured in war; blown up by mines; killed with weapons and armoury supplied by the arms traders. Can Micah's vision, that war and weaponry will be abolished from the land and people lie down in safety, yet find fulfilment?

If the words of Micah sound like a piece of wild optimism, try the Sermon on the Mount. There in Matthew 5.5 is the extraordinary statement: 'Blessed are the meek, for they shall inherit the earth.' It seems unlikely. However, the word for 'meek'[5] may best be rendered as 'powerless'; some suggest 'non-violent'. Blessed are the 'powerless', for they shall inherit the earth. Does that sound any more likely? Well – there might be a new twist to our understanding of that in a nuclear age. For it is certain that those who unleash the weapons of a nuclear arsenal cannot inherit the earth. The whole idea of nuclear deterrent is that it is a perilous game of bluff; for were the weapons ever to be used, they would destroy whatever anyone would care to defend. Weapons of such colossal destructive power cannot be weapons of defence. In vast stockpiles around the world there lie the weapons which cannot be used. To use them would be to invite destruction.

When we think of the cost of those weapons there seems to be in the policy of nuclear defence a kind of madness. Let us spend millions, billions of pounds on weapons we can never use. What a great idea! Yet it does really happen. Two years ago a new Trident submarine was launched. We now have four of them, and it is estimated that three million pounds of taxpayers' money is spent every day on those submarines. They have 96 warheads, and a destructive potential 3,000 times that of the bomb that destroyed Hiroshima. Conceived at the height of the Cold War for a situation that no longer exists, they are a very expensive symbol of British military virility. Even a senior British military figure was heard to say of the latest Trident, 'what on earth is the bloody thing for?' They are a colossal expense. But they can never be used, because if they were they could create a situation in which everything we ever cared to defend would be destroyed. Paradoxically, that huge, black, menacing thing is the ultimate white elephant. It cannot be used.

Only those who renounce the violence symbolized by Trident can inherit the earth. Could the Sermon on the Mount actually make sense? It is in that same passage we are told: 'Blessed are the peacemakers ; they shall be called God's children' (Matt. 5.9). Here, in the Sermon on the Mount, the peacemakers are told that they will be called God's children – those who are remade in the image of God.

Let's make a noise, as Christian peacemakers; let us raise our voices against the promiscuous sale of arms to anyone who wishes to buy them, with profits for the dealers the only consideration. Let us raise our voices for peace. Maybe we too can become peacemakers, and so be remade in the image of God.

19 Fifty Years of Peace

There have been many commemorations of the fiftieth anniversary of the end of the Second World War. For those of us who are old enough they will have awoken memories of a war which involved everybody, civilians and soldiers alike. For some, the memories brought to the surface will have been bitter. I recall a story of my father-in-law on a holiday in northern Italy several years ago, when he found his way to a large military cemetery. He stood and looked at the graves, and tears rolled down his face as he remembered comrades of the Eighth Army who had gone with him from North Africa to the allied invasion of Italy, and unlike him had not come home. The war was the cause of years of separation, of husbands and wives, mothers and sons, fathers and daughters, and even for those who did eventually return it must have been so hard to pick up again lives which had been torn apart by the hardships and hell of war.

An earlier generation experienced two world wars in quick succession which changed the face of Europe for ever. In the second of them civilians were brought into war in a new way, as aerial bombardment quickly came to target civilian populations and made of them a new front line. What seemed natural to those who grew up in the war would now seem abhorrent: the wail of the sirens as the bombers or the flying bombs headed for our neighbourhoods; the school classes that suffered constant interruption as children and teachers rushed for the shelters, to continue lessons there – how did we ever learn anything?; or the experience I recall of walking around the streets after flying bomb raids and looking with great curiosity, but not I think any real fear, at the piles of rubble, the staircases that often remained standing, and the digging for bodies in the ruins of the houses. For a young boy it was just how things were.

Fifty years on, we commemorated the end of the war and the beginning of a period of fifty years of peace. Although it has not quite been that, has it? The next generation of young men – the National Service generation – were involved in the Berlin air-lift, the Korean War, the wars of colonial withdrawal, and the Suez crisis, all of which happened within ten or eleven years of the end of the Second World War. We wondered how long it would be before the next major war. Between the First and Second World Wars there had been a gap of only twenty-one years. Had that pattern been repeated, we could have expected the next war by 1966.

Well, there was the Bay of Pigs crisis in 1962, when Kennedy and Kruschchev took the world to the brink of nuclear war. The Soviets had placed their missiles in Cuba in an attempt to balance American nuclear strategy. Material in the Kennedy Library's oral history record reveals the American assumption that they would have to invade Cuba. Dean Acheson told President Kennedy that Soviet missiles would have to be knocked out first. 'What will the Soviets do?' he was asked. 'Knock out our missiles in Turkey,' was the reply. 'What do we do then?' asked the President. 'Knock out a missile base in the Soviet Union.' That was a conversation which actually took place. For one weekend in 1962, a mere seventeen years after the Second World War, the world hovered on the brink of a third World War. Such a war would not have required conscripts; only targets for the macabre game of nuclear escalation. Fortunately, it didn't happen; and here we are, more than fifty years on from the Second World War.

In this country we have had no conscription since 1957; in mainland Britain no war involving the civilian population; no long separations of three, four, five years, as men went off to war and women and children stayed at home. It has been a great blessing, and is certainly something for which we give thanks.

How different our lives might have been. Peace. We have had peace.

In the light of that, however, we might think of a warning given by the prophet Jeremiah: 'They have healed the wound of my people lightly, saying "Peace, peace", when there is no peace' (6.14 RSV) We have had peace in mainland Britain. But we are aware of all the wars in which other people in other countries have been involved. We have had peace. But there have been well over three hundred wars around the world since 1945.[1] Some of them we know about, and know people who were involved. Korea and Suez have already been mentioned. More recently, the Falklands and the Gulf wars have been brought into our sitting rooms, the gory details of war now available on television, with action replays of the highlights. In addition there have been Britain's wars of colonial withdrawal – from Malaya, and Burma and Cyprus, and other places where National Servicemen had to fight as well as polish their boots, as Britain slipped away as quickly and quietly as possible from her colonial past. From time to time – at anniversaries or in film or theatre – we are reminded of America's colonial war in Vietnam, with images of helicopters whirling away from the rooftops of Saigon, carrying the fleeing Americans and a chosen few of their Vietnamese allies. There have been other wars, too, in Afghanistan and South America and the Congo and so many other places. More than three hundred wars altogether during the past fifty years. It is horrifying to contemplate how many people have suffered and died in wars around the world since 1945. We must be careful not to cry too easily, 'Peace, peace,' when there is no peace, lest we are accused of healing the wound of God's people lightly.

When Jeremiah first uttered those words, the powerful and threatening neighbours of Israel – Assyria and Mesopotamia – were themselves being threatened by the Scythians from beyond the Caucasus.[2] Jeremiah warned people that 'evil looms out of the north, and great destruction'.[3] His fellow-countrymen were not interested in his message; they had other more immediate concerns. 'For from the least to the greatest of them every one is greedy for unjust gain; and from prophet to priest, every one deals falsely' (6.13). It suited the leaders to utter soothing words, and to turn away from danger. Said Jeremiah: 'They have healed the wound of my people lightly, saying "Peace, peace", when there is no peace.' That, by the way, is an older translation of Jeremiah, in this case taken from the Revised Standard Version of the Bible. More modern versions have the people saying: 'all is well', to which Jeremiah replies, 'All well? Nothing is well.' Yet the Hebrew text clearly uses the word *shalom* – peace.[4] Shalom is the word of greeting used by Jesus to his disciples after the resurrection. Shalom is the word used by Jesus when he warned the people of Jerusalem of the dangers they faced if they did not heed his message of peace: 'If only you had known this day the way that leads to peace!' (Luke 19.42). Shalom can mean the total well-being of society, but it also means 'peace' in our own common use of the word; and since Jeremiah 6 is much concerned with the threat of war and destruction approaching from the north, it seems natural to use the word in that sense here. Jeremiah accuses the religious leaders of the day of being like worthless doctors who for the sake of their own ease assure their sick patients that they are well: 'They have healed the wound of my people lightly, saying "Peace, peace", when there is no peace.'

We have commemorated the end of a war. But we cannot simply cry, 'Peace, peace' if there is no peace. The construction and preservation of peace requires enormous effort, diplomatic skill, and incredible patience, as we see in Serbia, Bosnia and Croatia, as well as in Ireland. It also requires a public opinion that will not accept hostilities begun and continued in its name. Yet the churches have a mixed record in peacemaking. It is a strong temptation not to speak out on issues of war and peace, for fear of upsetting respectable members of congregations who put money in the collection and keep the wheels of church life turning. In our case, perhaps, not to heal a wound lightly, but to pretend we have never seen a wound. That is not an inevitable position, and thank God there have been many honourable exceptions to it.

Gathering material for a book on Mahatma Gandhi and Martin Luther King Jr.,[5] I had the pleasure of visiting Dr Harold DeWolf, one-time Professor of Theology at Boston University and supervisor of Martin King's PhD thesis. Martin Luther King had kept closely in touch with his old Professor, and turned to him for advice right up to the time of his own death in 1968. When he was considering whether or not to speak out publicly in opposition to the Vietnam war, Martin King telephoned Harold DeWolf, and the two met for dinner. They sat for hours afterwards in the car park discussing the pros and cons of a public statement from the civil rights leader on Vietnam.[6] The problem was obvious. Lyndon Johnson, the American President, had been a supporter of civil rights for blacks in the USA. It was he, not J. F. Kennedy, who had pushed legislation through Congress. But Lyndon Johnson, they knew, would not take kindly to criticism of his position on Vietnam. To speak against the war would be to risk alienating one of the most powerful supporters of civil rights. It might have been prudent to have kept quiet, like the prophets and priests of whom Jeremiah complained. That was not Martin Luther King's way. He became the first major church leader in the USA to speak out against the Vietnam war, and by doing so he added greatly to the swelling tide of public opinion against it. Christians have a responsibility to assume a role as peacemakers.

It is not an easy thing to do. We live in a society in which devotion to violence is deeply rooted. Much of our popular culture, our nationalism, our foreign policy is undergirded by a myth of redemptive violence, by the idea that revenge, particularly violent revenge, will be good for people. When there is a problem, let's hit out at something, hurt somebody. That'll teach them. It's a popular idea, and very seductive.

The early Christians seem to have recognized that there was a fundamental incompatability between the new order preached by Jesus and the society of their own day. One of the ways in which they kept that hope alive was to picture the return of Jesus. Later, Christians turned that on its head, moving away from a message of peace to a message of power. Walter Wink, an American biblical scholar, put it with nice irony when he wrote:

> The expectation of the return of Jesus functioned mythologically to keep alive the conviction that the values he incarnated would be vindicated in humanity's future. How ironic, and utterly predictable, that his return became weighed down with androcratic fantasies of revenge, violence, and autocratic rule, so that at his second coming Jesus would do everything he so resolutely refused to do at his first.[7]

Yearning for a messianic redeemer becomes a kind of totalitarian fantasy which can be fulfilled only in Hitler-like figures. Following the way of Jesus involves seizing the moral initiative; finding a creative alternative to violence; exposing the injustice of some of the systems under which we live; recognizing our own power to change things.

Our response to fifty years of a kind of peace, in a world in which it is all too easy to cry 'Peace, peace' when there is no peace, is to follow the vocation of the Christian peacemaker in a violent world.

Spirituality

20 Jesus at Prayer

What do you do when you are ill? I mean, seriously ill? I imagine that you call the doctor, or go to the surgery if you can manage the journey. If it is more serious than that, you call an ambulance and are then taken to hospital. There are people, of course, whose religious convictions lead them to look elsewhere for healing. We have all heard of Jehovah's Witnesses who have refused blood transfusions for themselves or their children because of their reading of certain biblical texts. And there are Christian evangelists who suggest that healing is to be obtained more effectively through faith than through medicine. Happily, I cannot now remember the name, but not long ago a transatlantic evangelist displayed posters of his meetings in this country showing discarded crutches and empty wheelchairs, presumably suggesting that his meetings could cure what modern medicine could not.

Do you believe it? Be honest! When you are ill, where do you look for help? Do you think first of faith and prayer, or of doctors and nurses? For my part, were I to be visited at my hospital bed by a surgeon who was to operate on me, my questions would not be, 'What do you believe?' 'Can I trust your religious faith?'; but 'Have you done this before?' 'Are you any good at it?' 'What is your success rate?'

One of my jobs in India many years ago was to run a correspondence course which produced material intended for non-Christians who wanted to read the New Testament with some degree of understanding. Sending out the material was a staff of six people who worked from a small set of offices in a large and dusty compound. One day a visitor had just approached the office when he had a minor epileptic fit. I tried to do what

I thought was appropriate, ensuring that he was not in danger of swallowing his tongue and that he was lying comfortably. But the staff rushed out, shouting to me that the man was possessed by a demon and that I should immediately exorcise him. Those men were devout Christians, of fairly limited education, but they knew their Bibles well. Certainly they had read Mark's Gospel, and the comment in the first chapter that '. . . they brought to him all who were ill or possessed by demons . . . He healed many who suffered from various diseases, and drove out many demons' (Mark 1.32–34).

They assumed that something of that sort was the first thing to do in the circumstances. Would we think like that? I doubt it! In that part of India there was an obvious alternative in a more enlightened form of Christian healing. Just down the road was the Medical College and Hospital in Vellore. The majority of staff were very committed Christians, and their work and their professional lives clearly reflected their Christian convictions. Many of them worked for a fraction of the salaries they might have commanded elsewhere. But they healed through modern medical science in an environment where they were supported and sustained by prayer. Their way of continuing the healing ministry of Jesus seemed to me to be by far the best way: to do it in the spirit of Jesus, with compassion and love and concern for the patients; not seeking rewards for themselves (the most distinguished consultants never received so much as a rupee from private patients, whose fees went into the hospital funds to pay for those who could not afford treatment). In that spirit they healed through the marvels of modern medical science. That was, and still is, authentic Christian healing; the kind of healing I assume we would wish for ourselves.

The Gospels include vivid scenes in which crowds press around Jesus, seeking help. They brought with them sick and frightened people, and Jesus healed some of them. There are Christians for whom a literal reading of material of that kind provides justification for faith-healing as a present-day alternative to modern medicine. Such an interpretation is neither necessary nor particularly helpful. Better to read such texts as suggesting the limitless compassion of Jesus for all those in need, expressed in ways appropriate to his own time and place. There may be a more telling focus, for our own spiritual needs, in the verses which follow Mark's accounts of the crowds who sought healing. The next picture is of Jesus escaping the pressure of the crowds: 'Very early in the morning Jesus got up and went out. He went away to a remote spot and remained there in prayer. But Simon and his companions went in search of him' (Mark 1.35f.).

The public ministry of Jesus had begun at Capernaum. Very quickly, in Mark's account, Jesus was caught up in strange happenings. There were healings and exorcisms which created great excitement and drew the crowds. The reaction of Jesus was to get up while it was still night and go out to a lonely spot to pray, no doubt reflecting in the process on that initial reaction to his ministry. Simon and his other close followers pursued him. The word used in the text means something like 'tracked him down' *katadiokein*; a pursuit in a hostile sense. If a reporter had been writing in Greek about the media pursuing a public figure involved in a sex scandal, it is just the word he would have used. They tracked Jesus down.

The story assumes that Simon and the others found it difficult to understand what Jesus was doing. The crowds were a sign that what Jesus was saying and doing was attracting attention. He was a success. For the disciples that must have been very gratifying. Here was a solid, measurable way of assuring themselves that what they were doing was right, and had public approval. Don't we all want that? Yet at the very moment when everything was going so well, Jesus went away to a lonely place where no one would see what he was doing, or be impressed by him. Perhaps that was because at a moment of stress Jesus wanted to get away from the crowds, and reflect and be quiet.[1] But it was also the natural reaction of a person with a cultivated religious sense. It was necessary to get away from the crowds and the attention which made it hard to focus on reality and to keep things in proportion.

Jesus at prayer; Jesus in solitude; Jesus silent. These were important parts of his life. The first chapter of Mark has already told of Jesus, after his baptism by John, going out into the wilderness for forty days. Almost six weeks alone in a hostile environment, in silence, with time to reflect and to pray. Then, almost immediately after his public ministry had begun and he had felt the initial reaction, he went off to be alone again. Jesus at prayer; Jesus in solitude; Jesus silent. This was not a sudden aberration; it was something central to his life and ministry.

In the Chinese classic, the *Tao-te ching*, there is a wonderful verse which says: 'He who speaks does not know; he who knows does not speak.' Those of you who have spent many hours sitting through synods or conferences listening to a succession of speakers with nothing to say may warm to that piece of wisdom. But it might seem an unlikely text for a preacher, or for religious and public traditions which put great store by public speaking. Well, think of it this way. If we spend all our lives chattering, how are we ever to understand anything? If we constantly need to be diverted, how can we ever focus on the things that really matter? There are times for speaking; but there are also times for being silent. There is a lesson in that for many kinds of worship, as well as for private reflection and prayer. Every now and again I take myself off to a Quaker Meeting, where it is often possible to have an hour of corporate but almost entirely silent worship. You sit with other people and are aware of their presence. But you are left to your own resources for most of the time. Each person needs to be able to sustain reflection or meditation for a considerable period of time. I have never been quite clear whether Friends are taught how to meditate, or whether they are expected to acquire as they go along the skills required to focus the mind for long periods. It does require training if one is to learn to be silent, and to reflect, and to pray. The followers of Jesus apparently noticed that, because it was 'after Jesus had been praying' that one of his disciples asked, 'Lord, teach us to pray' (Luke 11.1).

I am sure it is no accident that the forms of eastern religions which have become most popular in Britain are those that do teach people, quite formally, how to pray and meditate. Churches do very little of that, and silent prayer and meditation form only a tiny part of Christian worship. Indeed, much Christian worship appears to assume that people have to be constantly distracted, hectored, entertained or diverted. If after a Sunday or two of Quaker worship I return to more usual surroundings, I am often left thinking, 'Well, that was all very jolly; but when am I supposed to worship? When is there a rest from all these words that are constantly thrown at me?' I have even been to services on Remembrance Sundays when a two minutes' silence has been announced, and then a whole minute of it has been filled with the preacher telling the congregation what they should be thinking!

Against that background it is easy to understand how attractive it is for thoughtful people to go to a place – like a Friends' Meeting – where silence is the norm and the 'ministry' of members of the Meeting only a small part of the whole; or to a Buddhist Centre, where the teaching of meditation is basic to what is done; or to visit a Christian meditation centre, where encouragement is given to dip into the rich traditions of Christian spirituality. At one level, what is acquired may be little more than learning how to quieten the mind, to rid oneself of distractions, to focus the mind on one point. It is unlikely that it will have anything to do with asking for things. But it will be following the example of Jesus.

Jesus at prayer; Jesus in solitude; Jesus silent. In our own moments of silence we shall need to be comfortable; to breathe regularly and easily, and perhaps to associate our breathing in and out with the mental rehearsal of a simple prayer; and to have some suitable short phrases from scripture or from books of prayers to help us. Here are some examples:

> O God, of your goodness, give me yourself, for only in you have I all.

> You have made us for yourself, and our hearts are restless until they rest in you.

Lord Jesus Christ, the home we make for, the way we go by; help us to go by you, to you, so that we may not go astray.

Lord, we lie open before you, waiting for your healing, your peace, and your word.

For that is where the healing of our minds and spirits may come from, as we try to follow the example of Jesus, at prayer; in solitude; and silent.

21 Religious Pride

The New Testament contains much material critical of religious pride. Consider, for example, the following:

> As he taught them, he said, 'Beware of the scribes, who love to walk up and down in long robes and be greeted respectfully in the street . . . those who eat up the property of widows, while for apearance sake they say long prayers' . . . As he was sitting opposite the temple treasury, he watched the people dropping their money into the chest. Presently there came a poor widow who dropped in two tiny coins, together worth a penny. He called his disciples to him and said, 'Truly I tell you: this poor widow has given more than all those giving to the treasury; for the others who have given had more than enough, but she, with less than enough, has given all that she had to live on' (Mark 12.38, 41–44).

The passage begins with a criticism of religious leaders. So what's new? Archbishops and bishops, Chief Rabbis and Imams are easy targets for criticism. The Gospels contain an appreciable amount of material which depict Jesus criticizing the religious leaders of his day. One of the notable things about Jesus was how often and how harshly he criticized religious leaders, compared with his gentle and accepting approach to people others thought beyond the pale. The scribes, featured in this passage, were sometimes criticized by Jesus for their ostentatious piety, for making a great show of their religious zeal. And while that might seem to have been a bit silly of them, it doesn't appear to be the kind of thing that would have done great harm to anyone.

But in verse 40, notice, the scribes are criticized for eating up the property of widows while saying long prayers. The metaphors suggest rather a difficult set of manoeuvres, don't they? The point, of course, is that those who oppress the defenceless are guilty not only of failing to love God but also of failing to love their neighbour. Look further back in Mark 12 and you will see that this is reinforcing verses 28 to 34, where Jesus draws from Torah the great commandments to love God and love one's neighbour. The chapter fits together, and prepares for what is to follow in the story of the Passion of Jesus. But let's not leave 'those who eat up the property of widows' too quickly.

The likelihood is that in this situation Jesus was as much concerned with religious as with social wrong. The use of long prayers to extract cash might seem to be particularly offensive, whether in the time of Jesus or in our own time. There are zealous Christian evangelists – often American television evangelists – who make a direct connection between prayers, preaching and money. The appeal is: 'send your gift, and in return God will richly bless you'. Judging by the lifestyle of some of those who live by faith in this way, there are plenty of gullible people who fall for it. You can almost hear the rationalizing that goes along with such greed: 'if widows want to hand over their property to me, that's up to them; but let's pray that they will.' It's phoney, of course. And quite as unpleasant as the behaviour of those Jesus criticized. Yet in spite of all that, I want to suggest that the criticism as a whole is essentially a criticism of a particular kind of religious pride. It is a warning against the use of religion to boost the ego. Many of us use religion in that way.

In David Hare's play about a group of clergy, *Racing Demon*, one of the characters is a bishop who is presented as a good establishment figure and a poor pastor. Visiting a small group of variously troubled priests in the East End of London, he cannot help saying, 'These days they have me on Radio Four every Friday, you know,' and the unctious tone of the actor exactly reflected the style which is sadly too familiar. William Johnston, Catholic writer and perceptive Christian commentator on

Buddhism, writes about the way Japanese Buddhists think about the ego. There is a distinction between the 'small self' and the 'big self'. The small self (*shoga*) is what we build up by clinging to money and power and status, seeing ourselves as the one great reality of our world, and so building up a self which separates us from God, the universe, and other people. But there is another kind of self, the 'big self' (*taiga*) which is not thought of as something entirely separate from other people or from God. It is the same 'I', but with an expanded conciousness that can embrace everybody and everything. Johnston writes:

> When I lose the consciousness of separation and isolation in order to embrace the consciousness of the all, I am reaching a state that Buddhism calls emptiness and Christianity calls humility.[1]

May I sow the seed of a thought that this is what Jesus is at least partly concerned with here? Some of the things people do, even religious things – saying prayers, going to services, being a worthy church member – may be done in order to boost their own egos; to make themselves feel more important; to separate themselves off more from other people, and so (paradoxically) from God as well. But there is another way. Acting with detachment (it is difficult to think of a better word) we may continue to engage in prayer, worship, and service, but not in order to gain something for ourselves, for that little ego. Then we shall be less concerned with status, and more in touch with reality.

Jesus was fiercely critical of an obsession with status. We see that elsewhere in his life and teaching. He did not reject ambition, he simply changed the objects to which it is attached; he did not reject power, but he refused the use of power to dominate others; he did not reject greatness, but for him greatness was found in identification and solidarity with those at the bottom of society. What he did reject was attachment to status, and was strongly critical of those for whom status is everything. Jesus did his best to reject the titles people put upon him. Most New Testament scholars seem to agree that he did not claim for himself titles such as Son of God, Messiah, and certainly not the title 'God' – the kind of labels his followers attached to him later. Jesus told his disciples: 'you must not be called "rabbi", for you have one Rabbi, and you are all brothers . . . Do not call any man on earth "father", for you have one Father, and he is in heaven . . . the greatest among you must be your servant' (Matt. 23.8–11).

And did he not caricature, or even lampoon, the prevailing picture of Davidic kingship when he entered Jerusalem on a donkey, giving a farcical twist to one of the common ideas of the messiah as a conquering hero?[2] Jesus was critical of ideas of status, and tried to resist those who wanted to ascribe exulted status to him. But after his death he had no control over his followers, as they developed a christology which put him firmly back into a status-driven world. Is it appropriate to try to fit the figure of Jesus into a world of status? Or for his followers to set so much store by it?

Which leads us to the final verses, about the poor widow who dropped into the treasury 'two tiny coins, together worth a penny'. Now we are supposed to proclaim good news. But here first is some bad news. These verses are not saying it is fine, or admirable, to put a couple of tiny coins in the collection. Indeed, were we to look at the text in financial terms (a misunderstanding, I fear) it would be saying to us that we should empty our pockets and our wallets and put everything we have into the collection. The point, I suspect, is rather different. It has to do with the complete devotion of the poor widow, contrasted with the carefully calculated religious acts of the majority. In that sense, the poor widow's behaviour is a model of the values of the kingdom of God. Walter Wink makes a great deal of the ministry and teaching of Jesus as being opposed to domination, or to the use of power to control others. He claims that:

Ranking, domination hierarchies, and classism are all built on accumulated power provided by excess wealth . . . Breaking with domination means ending the economic exploitation of the many by the few. Since the powerful are not likely to abdicate their wealth, the poor must find ways of transcending the Domination Epoch while still in it.[3]

He gives a long list of examples and illustrations of how the New Testament text promotes such ideas. John the Baptist told people that if they had two shirts they should share with him who has none. Jesus poured scorn on those who wore soft raiment and lived in king's houses; he said that it is impossible to serve God and mammon; his followers were to live as if a new system was already in existence, and so they were sent out without food or clothing . . . and so on. We might reflect on that in the light of what appear to be astonishingly harsh words in the Letter of James.

> Next a word to you who are rich. Weep and wail over the miserable fate overtaking you: your riches have rotted away; your fine clothes are moth-eaten; your silver and gold have corroded, and their corrosion will be evidence against you and consume your flesh like fire.

Why should this be? Because, wrote James:

> The wages you never paid to the men who mowed your fields are crying aloud against you, and the outcry of the reapers has reached the Lord of Hosts. You have lived on the land in wanton luxury, gorging yourselves . . . You have condemned and murdered the innocent one, who offers no resistance (James 5.1–6).

Exploitation is at the heart of the matter. The poor widow is in her way a model of the values of the kingdom of God inaugurated by Jesus, who encouraged us to think in terms of a world in which status counts for nothing and all are valued for their true worth in the eyes of God. Paul Tillich, a twentieth-century German-American theologian of great originality, spoke of God as 'ultimate concern' and of religion as having to do with 'what concerns us ultimately'.[4] It might throw the definitions into sharper focus if they were turned into a question, such as, 'What would you give your life for?' Would we be willing to give our own lives for our child? our partner? a neighbour? a stranger? a cause? As we move along the spectrum the possibility of a positive reply becomes less and less likely. What is it that really concerns us ultimately? Tillich's point is that if we believe in God there is something in that belief which is of total, unlimited concern to us, unlike most of our other concerns, which are limited or temporary or conditional. To believe seriously in God is to be seized by a conviction that overrides everything else. So Mark speaks to us of the total devotion of the poor widow, whom he presents as a model of a truly religious response, concerned not with status or power but with what matters most to her; with what to her is more important than anything else in the world. That makes her a suitable model of the values of the kingdom and of what it is seriously to believe in God.

22 Suffering

Among the controversial sayings of Jesus are his words about loving our enemies: '. . . what I tell you is this: love your enemies and pray for your persecutors; only so can you be children of your heavenly Father, who causes the sun to rise on good and bad alike, and sends the rain on the innocent and the wicked' (Matt. 5.44f.).

In part those words of Jesus are controversial because in the demand to love our enemies they expect more than natural human responses allow. But is there another problem here? God causes the sun to rise on good and bad alike, and sends rain on the innocent and the wicked. Is that right? Is it just? In a just world should not the good be rewarded and the innocent punished? That appears to be what most people expect. It is frequently the case that in the face of a disaster people ask how God could possibly have allowed such a thing to happen. Beneath that question there lies a common objection to belief in God. The existence of pain and evil in the world seems to contradict the Christian notion of a good and loving God. It is said: 'If God were good, he would wish to make his creatures perfectly happy; and if God were almighty, he would be able to do what he wished. But the creatures are not happy: therefore either God is not good, or he is not omnipotent.' So runs the conventional objection which regards the existence of evil in the world as the main obstacle to belief in God. And pain and suffering are evil. Or are they?

Perhaps we need to clear some ground before coming to the heart of the problem. The first thing to say is that although none of us likes pain, it does have a beneficial side. It was contact with a leprosy hospital that impressed upon me what I had only vaguely known. Some kinds of pain serve a useful purpose. Patients suffering from leprosy often lost sensation in their hands and feet, and that led to other problems. Walking barefooted, as is customary in village India, they could tread on a piece of glass, or a rusty nail, and gradually work it into their foot without realizing what was happening. The wound might then get infected; and the end result might be a serious injury, or even sometimes the loss of the foot. It was the same when sensation was lost in the hands. No longer would the patient know when they picked up the small metal beaker of coffee whether or not it was burning their hand; even a simple act like trying to turning a handle that had become stiff could result in their applying more pressure than the hand could bear, and so result in injury. What saves the rest of us from those kinds of injury is pain. We know when we have trodden barefooted on a piece of glass, or when we pick up something hot from the oven; or when we are using too much force – it is the sensation of pain that tells us. There are beneficial qualities in pain.

There are also some kinds of suffering that although not beneficial might admit of logical explanation. For example, even an all-powerful and loving God could not be expected to do things that are contradictory. One of the greatest discoveries of early humans was surely the discovery of fire. Imagine a group of people gathered together in a cave, dark, damp and inevitably cold on a winter day even in central France; wrapped in animal skins, huddled together for warmth, but alert all the time for the approach of a bear or one of the other animals with whom they had to share the caves. Then they discovered how to make fire. How that must have transformed their lives! The fire kept them warm. It gave them light. And it drove away the bears! But the fire was also dangerous. If a child wandered too close and unsuspecting reached out a hand to the glowing flame, it would be burned. God could hardly be thanked for creating fire and yet also blamed every time a child approached the flame and was burned. There is a difference between attributing omnipotence to God, and expecting him to do things that are contradictory.

So it seems a bit hard to to say that the suffering which occurs in situations of extreme hunger and poverty, or in armed conflicts, is the fault of God rather than of the people who could solve such problems if they had a mind to do so. But in spite of that, the problems remain. People continue to suffer appalling pain; the most dreadful natural disasters occur; some have to suffer what appears to be a totally unfair burden of suffering. The great twentieth-century example of inexplicable suffering is the Holocaust, the extermination of six million Jews. Many Jewish people dislike the word 'holocaust' because it has a biblical meaning of 'sacrifice' or 'burnt offering' – something that might be pleasing, or at least acceptable, to God. They prefer the word 'shoah', which means devastation, ruin, or unaccountable tragedy. There is no way of accounting for the Shoah in either rational or religious terms. For the believer, the question that cries from the concentration camps is, why did God not stop that meaningless and appalling suffering? Jürgen Moltmann wrote: 'Where tens of thousands die a senseless death. all religious explanations of suffering turn to lies.'[1] Some pain and suffering we cannot explain.

An example of an attempt to wrestle with the question of how we are to deal with pain and suffering is found in the Book of Job, a wonderful mixture of prose and poetry. Job is a timeless figure. His story is for everybody, everywhere. The book has an exquisite first sentence: 'There lived in the land of Uz a man of blameless and upright life named Job, who feared God and set his face against wrongdoing.' Job is a person who has everything, but he is also a very good man.[2] Then he is struck by misfortune. One after another there come the four messengers with their accounts of disasters: the loss of all Job's oxen and donkeys; his sheep; his camels; and then, his sons and daughters. Each time the messenger repeats the dreadful litany: 'only I have escaped to bring you the news'. Job tore his cloak, shaved his head, and threw himself on the ground:

Naked I came from the womb,
naked shall I return whence I came.

The Lord gives and the Lord takes away;
blessed be the name of the Lord (1.21).

A truly religious response, one might think. Life and death
are alike in the hands of God, said Job. But then Job was struck
again, by a loathsome skin disease. His three good friends came
to comfort him. When they saw him from a distance, they did
not even recognize him. When they approached and knew it was
Job, they tore their cloaks, wept aloud, and then sat for seven
days and seven nights with their friend on the refuse heaps
outside the town, 'and none of them spoke a word to him, for
they saw that his suffering was very great' (2.13).

Is that not the only thing one can do in the face of intoler-
able suffering? To be with someone, but to be silent? It may be
hard to resist the temptation to give 'good advice'; but any
advice that could be given would be banal. What could be said
by the healthy visitor to the person dying painfully, or to the
prematurely bereaved? To sit in silence may be the only thing
to do. Job's friends did not remain silent indefinitely, of course.
In the end they had to speak. But in the story their words are
of no help to Job. And then – we race through the book – from
chapter 38 there is a marvellous poem that goes on for five
chapters, beginning with words addressed to Job by God: 'Who
is this who darkens counsel with words devoid of knowledge?'
In the end Job confesses: 'I have spoken of things which I have
not understood, things too wonderful for me to know . . .
Therefore I yield, repenting in dust and ashes' (42.3, 6).

That is the end. There is no slick solution. Such answer as
there is in Job is the answer of an agnostic. 'I do not know.'
There is an honesty and a humility about that. But we need
more than that. Do we find any more when we turn from Job
to the Gospels? The first thing to strike the reader of the Gospels
is that they provide a way of responding to suffering rather than
an answer to the problems; with an understanding of the ways
of God within which our experiences of pain and suffering may
be placed.

First we notice a clear denial in the Gospels that personal illness, pain or suffering is a direct consequence of the will of God. In John's Gospel there is described an incident in which Jesus and his disciples encountered a man who had been born blind. A common understanding of that time was that a person's suffering must be the direct consequence of his own sin, or fault. So here was a conundrum. The disciples asked, 'Rabbi, why was this man born blind? Who sinned, this man or his parents?' (John 9.2). Typically, Jesus did not allow himself to be drawn into speculative discussion. He did two things. First, he rejected the view that suffering can be attributed directly to God; and then he healed the man. The cause of much suffering around us might not admit of a satisfactory explanation, but the proper human response is to try to alleviate it. The best kind of Christian mission around the world has long recognized that, by building hospitals and providing health care wherever people were suffering for lack of them.

Is that not the appropriate response to other people's suffering? Most people would rather be healed than receive a satisfactory explanation of why they are ill. John's evocative story, and the call to faith to which it leads – 'I am the light of the world' – says something about suffering, but it does not explain why suffering occurs, or why it strikes some people so much more than others. What is clear is that God is not portrayed in the New Testament as a benign and indulgent parent who will always shield his children from suffering. God may be understood as what gives meaning and purpose to our universe. But he should not be so personalized as to be regarded as our personal defender against the perils, agonies and terrors of life.

So it is that in Matthew Jesus is quoted as saying that God 'causes the sun to rise on good and bad alike, and sends the rain on the innocent and the wicked' (5.45). God is not to be seen as a superbeing who can wave a magician's wand to remove our hurt and pain; but he can be seen as the love and hope which support in times of agony and fear. At the heart of the Christian picture is a crucified Jesus. A Jesus whom God did not save. A Jesus who cried out in his pain and his agony: 'My God, my God, why have you forsaken me?' That is just the way we might cry out in our anguish. How are we to understand or to make sense of what is happening to us? My God, my God, have you forsaken *me*? We remember that Jesus cried out like that. Simone Weil said of those words in the mouth of Jesus: 'There we have the real proof that Christianity is something divine.'[3] In the same vein, she wrote: 'The extreme greatness of Christianity lies in the fact that it does not seek a supernatural remedy for suffering, but a supernatural use of it.'[4]

What can one say, as one holds the hand of somebody dying slowly and painfully? Not that it is simply the result of blind chance. Not that it is their – or somebody else's – fault. Not that the omnipotence of God makes it certain that the disease was intended, even though we cannot say why. What we might say is something like this:

'I believe that God is known best and supremely as love; that he reveals himself to us as suffering love, and so is in this suffering with you; God as love is not a superperson who could wave a magician's wand to remove your hurt and pain; but his love is not something that will be withheld from you, as the miracle cure might be; his love will be with you throughout this experience and beyond.'

When George Matheson, a nineteenth-century minister of the Church of Scotland, learned that he was going blind he wrote a hymn. He later said that it was composed 'with extreme rapidity' and that at the time, 'I was suffering from extreme mental distress, and the hymn was the fruit of that pain.'[5] One of the verses has the words:

O light that followest all my way,
I yield my flickering torch to thee:
My heart restores its borrowed ray,
That in thy sunshine's blaze its day
May brighter, fairer be.

In the end it is in worship that paradoxes can be resolved. We have no slick and easy answers. But we do have the disclosure of God in Jesus Christ, who points us to a God of love who is in our pain and suffering with us.

23 The Wilderness and the Garden

On a beautifully clear day in 1977 I flew from New Delhi to London on an Air India flight. As we crossed from Asia into Europe the bridge joining the continents at Istanbul was clearly visible as a narrow, faint line 35,000 feet below. Somewhere between Karachi and Istanbul we flew over the desert. For mile after mile after hundreds of miles the landscape far below appeared empty, desolate and forbidding. There were sand and sand dunes, and rocky outcrops, but almost no vegetation. I reflected on the differences between the religions and cultures which arose in that kind of territory and those which emerged in the settled agricultural societies of India.

From the wilderness there came Judaism. The Bible reminds us of the people of Israel in the desert, led by Moses.[1] Judaism is a faith much influenced both by the desert and by the hope of a promised land, flowing with milk and honey. The story of that forty year journey through the desert remains a powerful and evocative one for Jewish people. It is a story of endurance; a story of an act of liberation in an escape from slavery which for Jews and Christians alike has become a picture of ultimate salvation. It is a story of a journey through the desert that led to an ages-long attachment to vineyards and olive groves and many other good things. Judaism grew up in the desert.

So too did Islam, the third of the three great Middle Eastern religions, emerging in the seventh century in the deserts of Arabia out of the proclamations of a prophet whose early life had been spent leading the caravans through the barren country between Mecca and Damascus. There is something about desert religions that makes them uncompromising and strong, reflecting perhaps the masculine, hierarchical, nomadic societies in which they first grew. In that respect, they are unlike faiths which developed in settled agricultural societies, where the woman and mother was so clear and important a symbol of the regeneration of life.

In the Gospels the ministry of Jesus is seen to begin in his encounter with John the Baptist – truly an uncompromising wilderness figure, in the line of Moses and some of the great prophets. And immediately after his baptism by John, Jesus had his own wilderness experience. Christians have long remembered and reflected upon that experience. In the early centuries of Christian faith there were many who tried to follow the example of Jesus in the wilderness by becoming desert hermits, denying themselves fiercely in the hope of refining and purifying themselves for a better life beyond. In a much more modest way, the wilderness experience of Jesus has served to inspire practices of fasting, especially during Lent. That is now taken much less seriously than once it was, although the observance of Ramadan by our Muslim friends is a reminder of the importance attached to fasting in many religious traditions. The wilderness experience continues to provoke reflection.

The Gospels say that: 'Full of the Holy Spirit, Jesus returned from the Jordan, and for forty days wandered in the wilderness, led by the Spirit and tempted by the devil' (Luke 4.1, 2). As part of that reflection, we picture Jesus going alone into the wilderness, denying himself food, and trying to come to terms with some of the great religious ideas which had grown up in that rugged, desolate terrain. Those of us who have visited Israel may be able to visualize the kind of scene the Gospel writers may have had in mind. Think of the area around the Dead Sea, with its sometimes suffocating heat and choking smell of sulphur; or of the sun-baked ruins on the top of the mountain at Masada, where Jewish nationalists remained in revolt against the powerful Roman army from AD66 to 74; or of the desert site of the Qumran community at the other end of the Dead Sea from Masada. All those sites can conjure up the desolation of the Judaean wilderness, almost frightening in its intensity. It is in that kind of terrain that Jesus is said to have spent forty days and nights contemplating his future.

The portrayal of Jesus in the desert dispels the notion that Jesus was a kind of divine robot, programmed to do whatever God had already decided for him. All the ingredients of real decision-making are present in the story of the temptations – doubt, perplexity, anxiety, uncertainty. Here is a picture of the truly human Jesus. The temptations, notice, are all prefaced by the phrase, 'If you are the son of God . . .' The 'if' is very important, connecting as it does Jesus' agony of indecision with our own vulnerability when we try to make our own decisions in critical moments. After the baptism by John, Jesus became aware of his own vocation. Or might he have been mistaken? And so that insidious 'if'. If . . . if you are the Son of God, you should be able to do amazing, remarkable things. Why not give it a try? But he did not. In response to the temptations that came into his mind in that lonely and barren place, he remembered the teaching of scripture and related it to his own circumstances. He recalled verses of Deuteronomy, set within the wilderness story of the people of Israel. 'If . . . if you are the Son of God, turn this stone into bread.' Wasn't there something in Deuteronomy about how the children of Israel had been desperately hungry, and how that experience had been seen as a lesson? Ah yes – 'he afflicted you with hunger and then fed you on manna which neither you nor your fathers had known before, to teach you that people cannot live on bread alone . . .' (Deut. 8.3).

Then in his mind's eye he saw all the kingdoms of the world, and felt how wonderful it would be if you could wield some real power. Surely that would be good for everybody else as well? Like many a political leader before and after him, he could persuade himself that he would not really enjoy the trappings of state; but he wouldn't mind putting up with them in the service of the people. But he remembered something else that is written in Deuteronomy: 'You are to fear the Lord your God, and serve him alone' (Deut. 6.13).

His thoughts turned to Jerusalem, and the great temple. That was the physical and spiritual centre of his religion, the place where his people worshipped, and the city where power was concentrated. Do something breathtaking there, and people will certainly know all about it! 'If . . . if you are the Son of God, throw yourself off the parapet of the temple'. That sounded dramatic enough. Then he remembered how that passage of Deuteronomy continued:

> You must not put the Lord your God to the test as you did at Massah . . . (Deut. 6.16).

In the dry and dusty wilderness the people of Israel had complained bitterly to Moses: 'Why have you brought us out of Egypt with our children and our herds to let us die of thirst?' (Ex. 17.3). By the rock at Horeb, Moses found water; and he called the place Massah and Meribah [test and dispute]. You must not put the Lord your God to the test. A pity, but there it was. No certainty would be given to him. He would have to act in faith and hope. So he came to his provisional conclusion. Notice how at the end of his story of the temptations, Luke says: 'Having come to the end of all these temptations, the devil departed, biding his time' (Luke 4.13).

Biding his time. It was by no means the end of temptation, and doubt, and uncertainty. If we reach the end of those things we are either not human or not alive. And Jesus was both. So ended the experience in the wilderness. Stark choices had been made in a barren landscape.

That is how it was for Jesus. But what are we to draw from all of this? Difficult as the experience had been for Jesus, and hard as it would be in the future, the wilderness experience was for him a necessary part of the journey towards more fertile land, from a desert to a garden. As for the children of Israel, so for Jesus, the journey to the promised land could be made only via the wilderness. The alternation between wilderness and garden is part of the biblical experience, as well as part of the experience of every person.

Jeremiah, referring to his people's experience of exile from their precious homeland and eventual return to it, wrote: 'A

people that escaped the sword found favour in the wilderness
... Again you will plant vineyards on the hills of Samaria, and
those who plant them will enjoy the fruit ... They will come
with shouts of joy to Zion's height, radiant at the bounty of the
Lord: the grain, the new wine, and the oil, the young of flock
and the herd. They will be like a well-watered garden' (Jer. 31.2,
5, 12).

The well-watered garden is a familiar image in the Old
Testament. That other people of the book whose origins lie in
the desert – the Muslims – also had their dreams of a garden.
The 'delights of paradise' described in the *Qur'an* include a
description of the righteous

> Reclining there upon soft couches, they shall feel neither the
> scorching heat nor the biting cold. Trees will spread their
> shade around them, and fruits will hang in clusters over
> them.[2]

Indeed, it was a Muslim dream of paradise as a beautiful
garden, with running water and leafy foliage, that inspired
mediaeval Christian writers – Dante and others – to speak in
similar terms.

For the children of Israel in the wilderness there was the hope
of the Promised Land, flowing with milk and honey; for people
living in a dry and dusty wilderness, there was the promise of
a garden. In biblical imagery, the desert will one day be transformed into a garden. 'The Lord has comforted Zion ... turning her wilderness into an Eden, her arid plains into a garden
of the Lord' (Isa. 51.3).

The same prophet, Isaiah, spoke in glowing terms about the
transformation of the desert as a sign that God was with his
people; for him, the transformation of the desert was a symbol
of salvation and deliverance:

> Let the wilderness and the parched land be glad, let the desert
> rejoice and burst into flower ... these will see the glory of
> the Lord and the splendour of our God ... for water will
> spring up in the wilderness and torrents flow in the desert

. . . instead of reeds and rushes grass will grow . . . the Lord's people, set free, will come back and enter Zion (Isa. 35.1, 2, 6, 10).

In that same biblical tradition, then, it is not too fanciful to see the journey from wilderness to garden as a metaphor for our own journeys. To believe that our own wilderness experiences, of loss, of pain, of disappointed hopes and failed relationships – whatever for us may be the desert, the wilderness, of life – can by God's power be transformed into gardens where we find comfort and peace and acceptance and love.

For Jesus, return from the wilderness meant an immediate involvement in the bustle and clamour of the crowds who gathered around him, but then left him and went away; it meant trying to convey to the few remaining disciples things they were desperately slow to understand; and after a few months or years of that there came another and more demanding wilderness experience, in betrayal and cross. Even that could not defeat the hope that God's love might renew the arid earth of our own endeavours with new life. John's Gospel records that 'Near the place where he had been crucified there was a garden, and in the garden a new tomb, not yet used for burial' (19.41). In the Gospel story even that most final of wilderness experiences, that of death itself, could not prevent the renewal, the resurrection, of God's love and purpose.

Conclusion

24 Parting Words

In Lent 1991 BBC Radio 4 broadcast a series of services on Sunday mornings for which they invited a series of preachers to address the theme: 'If you had only one sermon to preach . . .' The idea was that preachers would reveal what they thought to be the most important message they could deliver. The first service was at my local church in Haywards Heath and the preacher on that occasion was Colin Morris. I fear I cannot recall the subject of his sermon, or what it was he was burning to say, but I have remembered the theme of the series. 'If you had only one sermon to preach. . .' So here is a reflection, based on that idea and also on a passage from Matthew 9 about the call of Matthew and two controversial issues. In Matthew's Gospel we read:

> As he went on from there Jesus saw a man named Matthew at his seat in the custom-house, and said to him, 'Follow me'; and Matthew rose and followed him. When Jesus was having a meal in the house, many tax-collectors and sinners were seated with him and his disciples. Noticing this, the Pharisees said to his disciples. 'Why is it that your teacher eats with tax-collectors and sinners?' Hearing this, he said, 'It is not the healthy who need a doctor, but the sick. Go and learn what this text means, "I require mercy, not sacrifice". I did not come to call the virtuous, but sinners' (9.9–13).

Let's leave the call for a moment. The first of the two controversial questions arose as Jesus was having a having a meal in Matthew's house, where 'many tax-collectors and sinners were seated with him and his disciples'. We can imagine the scene; indeed, sadly, we could probably recreate it from some church situations: the pursed lips, the antagonistic looks, the judg-mental attitudes. The judgment took shape in a question: 'Why is it that your teacher eats with tax-collectors and sinners?' Jesus replied, 'It is not the healthy that need a doctor but the sick. Go and learn what this text means, "I require mercy and not sacrifice." '

That leads to the first point, which is a plea for *tolerance*. Is it revealing, I wonder, that the subject of tolerance is not one for which it is easy to find appropriate hymns and readings from the Bible? Religions, in many ways quite rightly, want to present their best sides to the world. They are not readily self-critical. But frequently that can become an exclusivism which too easily becomes arrogance and rejection. History is full of examples of religions doing that, for sadly all religions to a greater or lesser degree share that tendency. But to confine our-selves to Christian history, we remember the anti-Jewishness that has been a marked feature of much Christian preaching and teaching from very early times.

We remember the ways in which European history has been disfigured by persecution of Jews and the misrepresentation of Judaism from the fourth century onwards. We cannot forget the continuing entail of the Crusades,which may no longer seem to be much of an issue for Christians, but still burns in the memories of Muslims. We recall the association of certain kinds of Christian religion with colonialism, providing an ideology of superiority and triumphalism to undergird the technological and military superiority of European colonial powers.

Happily, there have always been exceptions. If you read Kenneth Cracknell's book about theologians and missionaries involved with other religions in the late nineteenth century, which he calls *Justice, Courtesy and Love*[1] you will see how all three of those qualities have been exhibited by the best examples of Christian missionaries; but also by church leaders, and scholars, and hosts of ordinary Christians who have refused to listen to the appeals of bigotry, and have indeed learned what it means to hear the words: 'I require mercy, not sacrifice'. There are fine examples of a tolerance which is not just a vapid acceptance of absolutely anything, but a generosity of mind and spirit towards those who differ in their interpretation or their practice.

The urgent need for tolerance is especially evident in situations of armed conflict, of war and peace. We know how often religion is ushered into the arena to give greater force to ethnic or national rivalries: in Ireland; in Bosnia, Croatia and Serbia; between India and Pakistan; in China and Tibet. Religion too easily becomes a badge for intolerance. Hans Küng was right to say that there can be no peace between nations without peace between religions.

'I require mercy, not sacrifice,' said Jesus, quoting from the prophet Hosea.[2] That verse was to play an important part in Judaism after the destruction of the temple. Temple sacrifice was not possible any more. But what was at the heart of sacrifice, the intention of sacrifice – to celebrate the justice and the mercy and the love of God – that was possible, with or without the temple. The verse also fits very nicely with Matthew's theology: that the love of one's neighbour is the fulfilment of the law. Frederick William Faber wrote in a hymn:

> But we make his love too narrow
>   By false limits of our own;
> And we magnify his strictness
>   With a zeal he will not own.

What would you say if you only had one opportunity to speak about Christian faith? I would say something about tolerance.

There was a second question addressed to Jesus, this time by disciples of John the Baptist. 'Why is it that we and the Pharisees fast but your disciples do not?' The reply firstly is that while Jesus is with his disciples, they should rejoice, not fast. Fasting, in any case, was not practised by everybody in Judaism. It was always an option.

Then Jesus went on to say something about the tradition, and the possibility of re-interpretation. 'No one puts new wine into old wineskins . . . they put new wine into fresh skins.' Jesus, we notice, was a critic of his own tradition. Clearly, he remained firmly within his own Jewish tradition – or perhaps one should say traditions, since the modern reading of it is that there were many Jewish traditions of the time. He was not, in his lifetime, the founder of a new religion, intent on breaking away from Judaism. He was a Jew, who gathered around him other Jews, and at a time when Judaism itself was quite fluid and varied, he criticized and re-interpreted the tradition. That leads to the second thing I would like to say if I had but one chance: don't be afraid to criticize, and analyse, and re-interpret the tradition. It has always happened, from the very earliest days of Christianity. The dangerous thing is when people who have re-interpreted Christianity in one particular form then say, that's it. No one can interpret any further. No more development. One of the things that strikes me particularly about the Gospels is the number of times Jesus is presented there not as a conventional conformist figure, but as a person who was constantly asking questions, constantly throwing the traditions back at people and asking 'what do you think that means?'

But, many church people will say, we are those who promote a particular tradition. We are, as it were, selling Christianity. How can we do that in a critical way? It can be done. A proper kind of self-criticism reveals an honesty that many expect from those who claim to deal with religious truth. I recall the occasions when I used to take groups of Open University students every year to the Regent's Park Mosque in connection with their course on *The Religious Quest*. Sometimes the guides who showed us around and answered questions were converts to Islam. They were often unduly defensive, scarcely able to mention aspects of Islam without at the same time criticizing Christianity. The students – some Christian, most not – noticed the defensiveness. One year, however, we had the pleasure of being guided by the Imam himself. He was relaxed, open, not put out by questions apparently critical of Islam. And everybody was delighted! It is a willingness to question, to reexamine, to be honest about difficulties which shows real integrity. And significantly, when we do that with the traditions around Jesus we are actually employing the method of Jesus himself, being critics of the tradition in which we stand in order to take that tradition forward, to glimpse a light for our own day in a message that is ageless.

Why do we disciples of John the Baptist and the Pharisees fast, and your disciples do not? But you don't have to fast, Jesus replied. It is not a requirement. Are you not wasting that good new wine by pouring it only into those old brittle wineskins? Enlarge your minds. Open your imaginations.

I think most Christians would be astonished if they knew how wide and varied were the interpretations of Christian faith during the first three or four centuries of the church. The new heresies are actually the ones which claim that faith has always been the same. If I had one last chance to speak about Christianity I would want to say, always approach your tradition critically, after the manner of Jesus of Nazareth.

Finally, consider Matthew 9.9: Jesus saw a man named Matthew at his seat in the custom-house, and said to him: 'Follow me.' And Matthew rose and followed him. Isn't that remarkable? Doesn't it strike you as extraordinary? Jesus saw a man, and spoke two short words to him. The man got up, left his work, his livelihood, possibly his family and certainly his home, and went off to follow Jesus.

Could it have happened just like that? I doubt it. But that is the point. The abbreviation of the text; the deliberate heightening of the abrupt nature of the call, is saying something very important about Christianity. Exactly the same thing happens in Mark 1.16–20. First Simon Peter and Andrew, and then James and John, are called to be disciples in just the same abrupt way; and without a moment's hesitation, they follow. Christian faith is like that, the texts suggest. And that is the third thing I would want to say with a last opportunity – Christian faith is like that.

Not, of course, that someone will accost you as you leave church one Sunday morning and say, follow me, and you will go, leaving wife, mortgage and children without a second thought. But rather that, in philosophical terms, Christian faith is existential. That is, it emphasizes the uniqueness and unpredictability of human life; it emphasizes our freedom to choose and to act in unpredictable ways; in the words of one of the existentialist theologians, Rudolph Bultmann, it is to regard faith as *authentic existence*. To have faith is to know in ourselves what it means for Jesus to say, *I have come that they might have life, and have it in all its fullness.*

Kierkegaard, Danish philosopher and Christian thinker, regarded as the father of Christian existentialism, wrote: 'The subjective acceptance is precisely the decisive factor; . . . an objective acceptance of Christianity is paganism or thoughtlessness.'[3] Yet many Christians still think that the important thing is to read a statement of beliefs, and then sign on the dotted line to register their agreement. According to Kierkegaard, that is paganism or thoughtlessness. The subjective acceptance is precisely the decisive factor.

So the Gospel stories of how people became disciples are not lengthy records of manuals of instruction that had to be devoured, of long training sessions by the lake, of examination by an expert before admission to the role of disciple. No. They are stories in which the call is encapsulated in two words: 'Follow me.' They were the first words spoken by Jesus to Peter, Andrew, James, John and Matthew. According to John's Gospel, they were the last words addressed to Peter, when after the resurrection Peter was restored to a position of trust. It is by following in the footsteps of Jesus, again and again and again, that one discovers what it is to follow Jesus.

The same call comes to us. And as Albert Schweitzer wrote at the end of his *The Quest of the Historical Jesus*:

He speaks to us the same word: 'Follow thou me!' . . . He commands. And to those who obey Him, whether they be wise or simple, He will reveal Himself in the toils, the conflicts, the sufferings which they shall pass through in His fellowship, and, as an ineffable mystery, they shall learn in their own experience Who He is.[4]

There, in a final statement, are three qualities for Christians to cherish: tolerance; criticism; and response.

Notes

Preface

1. The decline is in terms both of the length of the training (shortened in many cases because of the increasing age of ordinands) and of the failure to learn such basic things as biblical languages. Whilst it would be unthinkable to have Muslim imams or Jewish rabbis who could not read the texts of their traditions in the original languages, it is increasingly common to find recently-trained Christian ministers who cannot do this.

1. Nothing Abides

1. St Teresa of Avila, *Nada te turbe*, translated from the Spanish by Colin Thompson.
2. Richard Bach, *Jonathan Livingston Seagull*, Pan Books 1973.

2. Wrestling with Contradictions

1. Wendy Doniger O'Flaherty, *Siva – the Erotic Ascetic*, OUP 1981, p.35.
2. Morna D. Hooker, *The Gospel According to St Mark*, A. & C. Black 1991, p. 344.
3. Simone Weil, *Gravity and Grace*, Routledge 1987, p. 22.

3. Christian Existentialism

1. For a brief definition of 'existentialism', see Raymond Williams, *Keywords*, Collins Fontana 1976, pp.122–25. For a discussion of Christian existentialism, see John Macquarrie, *An Existentialist Theology*, SCM Press 1955.
2. Raymond Williams, op. cit., p.124.
3. Jürgen Moltmann, *Theology of Hope*, SCM Press 1967, p.302.
4. *The Journals of Keirkegaard 1834–1854*, tr. Alexander Dru, Collins Fontana 1958, p.174. The whole passage reads: 'The moment I take Christianity as a doctrine and so indulge my cleverness or profundity or my eloquence or my imaginative powers in depicting it: people are very pleased; I am looked upon as a serious Christian. The moment

I begin to express existentially what I say, and consequently to bring Christianity into reality: it is just as though I had exploded existence – the *scandal* is there at once.'

4. On Being an Intelligent Christian

1. John A. T. Robinson, *Honest to God*, SCM Press 1963.
2. Raimundo Panikkar, *The Silence of God. The Answer of the Buddha*, Orbis Books, Maryknoll 1990, p.144.
3. Dionysius the Areopagite, *Opera*, J. P. Migne PG, 3, 1065a, quoted in Pannikar op. cit., p.205, n.74. Pannikar wrote: 'If someone, seeing God, knew what he saw, he did not see God,' said Denis the Areopagite, and with him, the greatest part of Christian tradition.
4. Raymond Williams, *Keywords*, p.170.
5. Brihadaranyaka Upanishad, 1, iii, 28.
6. Williams, ibid..

5. Believing in God

1. Peter Brierley, *'Christian' England. What the English Church Census Reveals*, Marc Europe 1991.
2. The translation is that found in *The Psalms – A New Translation for Worship* used in The Alternative Service Book of the Church of England, 1980, and the Methodist *Hymns and Psalms*, 1983.
3. D. Z. Phillips, *From Faith to Fantasy*, Macmillan 1991, p.205.
4. William Temple, *Readings in St John's Gospel*, first series, Macmillan 1941, p.18.
5. See Mark 10.18, where Jesus responds to the greeting 'Good Teacher' by saying, 'Why do you call me good? No one is good except God alone.'

6. Creative Spirit

1. See John 3.8.
2. John V. Taylor, *The Go-Between God*, SCM Press 1972, p.43.
3. Ibid., p.46.
4. In the translation by Dorothy L. Sayers (Penguin Classics), quoted by Taylor, ibid., p.46.
5. Ibid., p.47.

7. Why Seek the Living among the Dead?

1. Words by Cecil Frances Alexander, 1818–1895.
2. I. Howard Marshall, *The Gospel of Luke. A Commentary on the Greek Text*, The Paternoster Press 1978, p.883.

8. *Why Did Jesus Die?*

1. See Kenneth Grayston, *The Gospel of John*, Epworth Press 1990, p.22.
2. Rom. 3.25: 'God designed him (Jesus) to be the means of expiating sin by his death, effective through faith. God meant by this to demonstrate his justice . . .'
3. In Helen Waddell, *Peter Abelard*, Constable 1933, p.295.
4. For an extended treatment of these ideas, see S. G. F. Brandon, *Jesus and the Zealots*, Manchester University Press 1967.
5. Dietrich Bonhoeffer, *Letters and Papers from Prison*, The Enlarged Edition, SCM Press 1971, p.381. 'It is only this "being there for others", maintained till death, that is the ground of his omnipotence, omniscience and omnipresence.'
6. 10 April 1995. Bonhoeffer was executed on 9 April 1945.

9. *On Not Clinging to Jesus*

1. No. 720 in *Hymns and Psalms*, MPH 1983.
2. C. K. Barrett, *The Gospel According to St John*, SPCK 1955, p.470.
3. See Roger Hooker, *Themes in Hinduism, and Christianity*, Verlag Peter Lang, Frankfurt am Main 1989, ch. 5.

10. *Salvation*

1. Morna Hooker, *The Gospel According to St Mark*, p.388.
2. See Martin Forward, 'Salvation! O the joyful sound?', *The Expository Times*, 104/2, October 1992.
3. No. 216 in *Hymns and Psalms*.
4. No. 434 in *Hymns and Psalms*.
5. John Wesley, *A Plain Account of Christian Perfection*.
6. *The Works of the Rev. John Wesley*, Wesleyan Methodist Bookhouse 1881, Vol. XIII, p.197. I am indebted to Frank Whaling's paper 'Wesley's Premonitions of Inter-Faith Dialogue', presented at a Conference on *The Contribution of Methodists to the Academic Study of Religions*, Westminster College, Oxford, March 1994, for insight into this interpretation of the Wesleys.
7. Isaiah 61.1–2, quoted in Luke 4.18, 19.

11. *What is Scripture?*

1. Salman Rushdie, *The Satanic Verses*, Viking 1988, pp. 363–68.
2. Wilfred Cantwell Smith, *What is Scripture?*, SCM Press 1993.
3. From the *Mishnah*. Quoted and translated by Wilfred Cantwell Smith, op. cit., p.23.

4. C. S. Rodd, 'The Use of the Old Testament in Christian Ethics' in C. S. Rodd (ed) *New Occasions Teach New Duties*, T. & T. Clark 1995, pp.5f.

5. Isaiah 29.13f.: 'Because this people worship me with empty words and pay me lip-service while their hearts are far from me, and their religion is but a human precept (a commandment of men – RSV) learned by rote, therefore I shall shock this people yet again . . .'

6. See Morna Hooker, *The Gospel According to St Mark*, pp.173–81. Hooker says of the preference of Jesus for moral rather than ritual purity: 'The saying is a radical one, since it challenges the attitude which treats all the commandments on an equal level, and in doing so stands in the prophetic tradition' (p.179).

12. *Christianity – One Faith or Many?*

1. A theory I first committed to print in 1987 in 'Religion in the Modern World', the concluding chapter of Peter Bishop and Michael Darton (eds), *The Encyclopedia of World Faiths*, Macdonald/Orbis 1987.

2. J. E. Lesslie Newbigin, *A South India Diary*, SCM Press 1951, p.24.

13. *The Decade of Evangelism in the Light of Several Decades of Dialogue*

1. *The Guardian*, 12 February 1992.

2. Eugene Stockwell, *International Review of Mission*, July/October 1989.

3. William Johnston, *Letters to Contemplatives*, HarperCollins Fount 1991, pp.24, 25.

4. Vincent J. Donovan, *The Church in the Midst of Creation*, SCM Press 1989, p.116.

14. *The Rainbow*

1. T. S. Eliot, Choruses from 'The Rock', X, *Collected Poems 1909–1962*, Faber 1963, 1974, p.185.

2. For example, in the debate between Sadducees and Pharisees on the subject of resurrection. See Matt. 22.23–33, Mark 12.18–27.

3. E. P. Saunders, *Jesus and Judaism*, SCM Press 1985, p.199.

4. D. H. Lawrence, *The Rainbow*, Penguin 1974, p.496.

15. *The Landowner and the Vineyard*

1. 'The cultivating peasants . . . were exposed to the rods of the zamindars as the zamindars were liable to the rods of the government

officers, but like the zamindars themselves they had a traditional hereditary right and were rarely dispossessed . . . (under the British) he was sold up in a civilized British way instead of being beaten up but left where he was in the Mughal way': Percival Spear, *A History of India*, Vol 2, Penguin 1965, pp.96f.

2. See Morna Hooker, *The Gospel According to St Mark*, p.274.
3. I am indebted to the reflection on Camus' novel in David Anderson, *The Tragic Protest*, SCM Press 1969, ch. 5, 'The Sisyphean Hero'.
4. Albert Camus, *The Plague*, Penguin 1960, pp.213–4.

16. *Racial Justice in an Unequal World*

1. Rudyard Kipling, 'Recessional', written in 1897.
2. S. Allen, *New Minorities, Old Conflicts: Asian and West Indian Migrants in Britain*, Random House, New York 1971, p.46; E. J. B. Rose, *Colour and Citizenship*, OUP 1969, p.72; Commission for Racial Equality, *Fact Paper 2. Immigration – numbers and dispersal*, 1978. See also Peter D. Bishop, 'Victorian Values? – Some Antecedents of a Religiously Plural Society' in R. Hooker and J. Sargant (eds), *Belonging to Britain: Christian Perspectives on Religion and Identity in a Plural Society*, CCBI 1991.
3. See also Rom. 10.12 and Col. 3.11.

17. *War and Peace*

1. See C. K. Barrett, *The Gospel According to St John*, pp.473, 391.
2. Stanley Wolpert, *A New History of India*, OUP, 3rd edn 1989, p.334.
3. For an exploration of some of the curiosities of British attitudes to immigration, see my 'What Light Does the Jewish Experience Shed on the Idea of Multi-Cultural Britain?' in Y. Bauer et al (eds), *Remembering for the Future*, Pergamon Press 1989 and 'Victorian Values? Some Antecedents of a Religiously Plural Society' in R. Hooker and J. Sargant (eds), *Belonging to Britain*.
4. Herbert Butterfield, *Christianity, Diplomacy and War*, Epworth Press 1953. 3rd edn; Wyvern Books 1962, p.38.
5. President Reagan, at the time of the Gulf War.
6. Gandhi's assassination occured on 30 January 1948, four months after Indian Independence.

18. *A Peace Dividend?*

1. There is also a possibility that military equipment intended for Iraq was supplied via Jordan. 'There is, in my opinion, no doubt but that the

supply to Jordan of military equipment represented a potential means of breach of the Government's restrictive policy on supply of equipment to Iraq' (Lord Justice Scott in the Scott Report, quoted in *The Guardian*, 16 February 1996).

2. Will Hutton, *The State We're In*, Jonathan Cape 1995.
3. In February–March 1995.
4. 'In the world as a whole, at least 1 in 4 of all the scientists and engineers working on research and development are working on weapons. World spending on military research and development is rising much faster than military spending as a whole' (John Turner and SIPRI, *Arms in the '80s. New Developments in the Global Arms Race*, Taylor and Francis 1985, p.4).
5. *hoi praeis.*

19. Fifty Years of Peace

1. In 1983 Michael Kidron and Dan Smith in *The War Atlas. Armed Conflict, Armed Peace*, Pan Books/Pluto Press, claimed that 'There have been about three hundred wars since 1945. There has been no single day free of war and few islands of tranquility.'
2. 'The historical background of the book of Jeremiah is the period of the decline of Assyrian power and the rise of the Babylonian empire (*c.*640–570). During that period Judah enjoyed its last few decades of relative independence, came under the suzerainty of Egypt and then Babylon, disintegrated and collapsed as a nation state. Two invasions by the Babylonians led to deportations and the destruction of Jerusalem. It was a period which began with great chauvinism and expansionist policies maintained by King Josiah, but ended with the complete humiliation of territory, people and cities' (Robert P. Carroll, *From Chaos to Covenant*, SCM Press 1981, p.21).
3. Jer. 6.1. See also 6.22–26.
4. The Jerusalem Bible (1968) has: 'They dress my people's wounds without concern: "Peace! Peace!" they say, but there is no peace.'
5. *A Technique for Loving. Non-Violence in Indian and Christian Traditions*, SCM Press 1981.
6. Interview with Dr Harold DeWolf, Lakeland, Florida, 29 July 1980.
7. Walter Wink, *Engaging the Powers. Discernment and Resistance in a World of Domination*, Fortress Press, Minneapolis 1992, p.61.

20. Jesus at Prayer

1. See D. E. Nineham, *Saint Mark*, Penguin 1963, pp.83, 84.

21. *Religious Pride*

1. William Johnston, *Letters to Contemplatives*, HarperCollins Fount 1991, p.68.
2. Walter Wink describes the entry of Jesus into Jerusalem on an ass as a lampooning of Davidic Kingship by 'paradoxical reversal' (*Engaging the Powers*, p.113).
3. Ibid., pp.113, 114.
4. Paul Tillich, *Systematic Theology*, Vol. 1, James Nisbet 1953; SCM Press 1978, p.234.

22. *Suffering*

1. Jürgen Moltmann, quoted in 'Theodicy' in Alan Richardsom and John Bowden (eds), *A New Dictionary of Christian Theology*, SCM Press 1983, p.565.
2. The story is in its way an artifice, but that is how it makes its point. Cyril Rodd says of the opening verses: 'The picture of Job is extravagant . . . Too good to be true? In some ways perhaps it is. And yet we shall completely misread the rest of the book unless we take this description of his life seriously' (C. S. Rodd, *The Book of Job*, Epworth Press 1990, p.6).
3. Simone Weil, *Gravity and Grace*, Routledge 1987, p.79.
4. Ibid., p.xxvi.
5. Quoted in Richard Watson and Kenneth Trickett, *Companion to Hymns and Psalms*, MPH 1988, p.389.

23. *The Wilderness and the Garden*

1. See, for example, Deut. 6.1–17.
2. *Qur'an*, 76.14, tr. N. J. Dawood in *The Koran*, Penguin 1970.

24. *Parting Words*

1. Kenneth Cracknell, *Justice, Courtesy and Love. Theologians and Missionaries Encountering World Religions, 1846–1914*, Epworth Press 1995.
2. Matt. 9.13, quoting Hosea 6.6, which the Jerusalem Bible translates as: 'what I want is love, not sacrifice; knowledge of God, not holocausts.'
3. Søren Kierkegaard, *Postscript*, quoted in Robert Burtell (ed), *A Kierkegaard Anthology*, Princeton University Press 1973, p.103.
4. Albert Schweitzer, *The Quest of the Historical Jesus*, ET 1910; 3rd edn, A. & C. Black 1954; reissued SCM Press 1981, p.401.